∘ 2500 YEARS OF ∘

WISDOM

SAYINGS OF THE GREAT MASTERS

COMPILED BY

D.W. BROWN

DIVINE
ARTS

Published by DIVINE ARTS
DivineArtsMedia.com

An imprint of Michael Wiese Productions
12400 Ventura Blvd. # 1111
Studio City, CA 91604
(818) 379-8799, (818) 986-3408 (Fax)
www.mwp.com

Cover design by Johnny Ink www.johnnyink.com
Cover art by Matt W. Moore www.mwmgraphics.com
Copyediting by Annalisa Zox-Weaver and Matt Barber
Book layout by Gina Mansfield Design

Printed by McNaughton & Gunn, Inc., Saline, Michigan
Manufactured in the United States of America

Library of Congress Cataloging-in-Publication Data

Brown, D.W., 1956- compiler.
  2500 years of Wisdom : Sayings of the Great Masters /
Compiled with an Introduction by D.W. Brown.
     pages cm
  ISBN 978-1-61125-014-5
  1. Conduct of life--Quotations, maxims, etc. 2. Wisdom-
-Quotations, maxims, etc. 3. Anecdotes. I. Title. II. Title: Two
thousand-five hundred years of Wisdom.
  PN6084.C556B76 2013
  081--dc23
                                            2012040692

Printed on Recycled Stock

Table Of Contents

PREFACE
by
D.W. BROWN

A great quotation can deliver a shot to the heart much like a great work of art, presenting an unassailable truth that stings and delights simultaneously, a taste of a world unto itself — but still entirely about this one. Each of these quotations resonated with me in that way, serving to inspire, challenge, mature, and give solace; and, having collected the best of the best over many decades, I felt it my duty somehow to arrange them, perhaps as a naturalist might gather his specimens, kind with kind. I have attempted to construct a mosaic of concepts, a symphony of thought. You will find here, among writers of perhaps less renown, authors of widely recognized genius, who have historically instructed us how to value existence and make better our way. And, while appreciating the voices absent in our literature because they were lost, destroyed, or constrained — as with countless female writers through the ages — you might, as I have, look upon these intermingled quotations as a kind of manual for living.

Or not. It seems many of our greatest thinkers want little more than to tell us to stop overrating our thinking. Maybe you'll find in this book simply a collection of beautiful sentiments whose worth is purely in the pleasure of reading them. The truth is, I'm guessing you will encounter nothing here you didn't already know. But how wonderful and how affirming it is to remember you knew it!

I.

ONWARD

Do your work.

~ *Plato*

Know yourself and nothing too much.

~ *Plutarch*

Sustain and abstain.

~ *Epictetus*

See golden days, fruitful of golden deeds,
With joy and love triumphing.

~ *John Milton*, Paradise Lost

You are younger today than you will ever be again.

~ *Anonymous*

You'll break the worry habit the day you decide
you can meet and master the worst that can happen to you.

~ *Arnold Glasow*

Today is the first day of the rest of your life.

~ *Anonymous*

Until death, it is all life.

~ *Miguel de Cervantes*

To want to be free is to be free.

~ *Ludwig Börne*

Great flame follows a tiny spark.

~ *Dante Alighieri*, The Divine Comedy

Whatever man does he must do first in his mind.

~ *Albert Szent-Györgyi*

Sow a Thought, Reap an Act,
Sow an Act, Reap a Habit,
Sow a Habit, Reap a Character,
Sow a Character, Reap a Destiny.

~ *Ralph Waldo Emerson*

Affirmation of life is the spiritual act by which man ceases to
live thoughtlessly and begins to devote himself to his life with
reverence in order to give it true value. To affirm life is to deepen,
to make more inward, and to exalt the will to live.

~ *Albert Schweitzer*

Here we stand between two eternities of darkness.
What are we to do with this glory while it is still ours?

~ *Gilbert Murray*

Withdraw into yourself and look. And if you do not
find yourself beautiful yet, act as does the creator of a
statue that is to be made beautiful: he cuts away here,
he smoothes there, he makes this line lighter, this
other purer, until a lovely face has grown upon his work.

~ *Plotinus*

You cannot run away from a weakness;
you must some time fight it out or perish;
and if that be so, why not now, and where you stand?

~ *Robert Lewis Stevenson*

Perhaps the most valuable result of all education
is the ability to make yourself do the thing you have to do,
when it ought to be done, whether you like it or not.

~ *Thomas Huxley*

Do what you have to do, so you can do what you want to do.

~ *Anonymous*

You gain strength, courage, and confidence by every experience
in which you really stop to look fear in the face....
You must do the thing you think you cannot do.

~ *Eleanor Roosevelt*

You will make all kinds of mistakes; but as long as you
are generous and true, and also fierce, you cannot
hurt the world or even seriously distress her.
She was made to be wooed and won by youth.

~ *Winston Churchill*

To change one's life:
a. Start immediately
b. Do it flamboyantly
c. No exceptions
Never suffer an exception to occur
till the new habit is securely rooted.

~ *William James*

Motivation is what gets you started.
Habit is what keeps you going.

~ *Jim Ryuh*

Choose always the way that seems the best,
however rough it may be;
custom will soon render it easy and agreeable.

~ *Pythagoras*

Take risks: if you win, you will be happy;
if you lose, you will be wise.

~ *Anonymous*

Dare to be wrong and to dream.

~ *Frederick Schiller*

He who has never failed somewhere,
that man can not be great.

~ *Herman Melville*

If you're never scared or embarrassed or hurt,
it means you never take any chances.

~ *Julia Sorel*

Do not be too timid and squeamish about your actions.
All life is an experiment. The more experiments
you make the better. What if they are a little coarse,
and you may get your coat soiled or torn? What if
you do fail, and get fairly rolled in the dirt once or twice?
Up again, you shall never be so afraid of a tumble.

~ *Ralph Waldo Emerson*

If you woke up breathing, congratulations!
You have another chance.

~ *Andrea Boydston*

On the mountains of truth you will never climb in vain:
either you will get up higher today or you will exercise your
strength so as to be able to get up higher tomorrow.

~ *Friedrich Nietzsche*

Judge each day not by the harvest you reap
but by the seeds you plant.

~ *Robert Louis Stevenson*

You don't learn holding your own in the world
by standing on guard, but by attacking, and getting well
hammered yourself.

~ *George Bernard Shaw*

Do something every day for no other reason than
you would rather not do it, so that when
the hour of dire need draws nigh, it may find
you not unnerved and untrained to stand the test.

~ *William James*

We lose the fear of making decisions, great and small,
as we realize that should our choice prove wrong
we can, if we will, learn from the experience.

~ *Bill W.*

Besides the practical knowledge which defeat offers,
there are important personality profits to be taken.
Defeat strips away false values
and makes you realize what you really want.

~ *William M. Marston*

When he is pushed, tormented, defeated, he has a
chance to learn something; he has been put on his wits, on
his manhood; he has gained facts; learns his ignorance; is
cured of the insanity of conceit; has got moderation and real skill.

~ *Ralph Waldo Emerson*

Adversity introduces a man to himself.

~ *Albert Einstein*

He knows not his own strength that hath not met adversity.

~ *Ben Johnson*

Originality and a feeling of one's own dignity
are achieved only through work and struggle.

~ *Fyodor Dostoevsky*

There are defeats more triumphant than victories.

~ *Michel de Montaigne*

Times of general calamity and confusion have
ever been productive of the greatest minds.
The purest ore is produced from the hottest furnace.

~ *Charles Caleb Colton*

If you will call your troubles experiences,
and remember that every experience develops some
latent force within you, you will grow vigorous and happy,
however adverse your circumstances may seem to be.

~ *J. R. Miller*

A man can get discouraged many times,
but he is not a failure until he begins
to blame somebody else and stops trying.

~ *John Burroughs*

In the difficult are the friendly forces,
the hands that work on us.

~ *Rainer Maria Rilke*

Problems are messages.

~ *Shakti Gawain*

You may not realize it when it happens, but a kick in the teeth
may be the best thing in the world for you.

~ *Walt Disney*

Much of what we call evil is due entirely to the way men
take the phenomenon. It can so often be converted into a bracing
and tonic good by a simple change of the sufferer's inner attitude
from one of fear to one of fight; its sting so often departs and turns
into a relish when, after vainly seeking to shun it, we agree to face
about and bear it cheerfully.

~ *William James*

Would you still want to be born if you knew
ahead of time the cost for this life would be
all the inconveniences and discomforts you're going
to have to endure? Almost certainly you would,
and the problem is, because you weren't given that
list up front, you find yourself acting
as if it was all supposed to be free. But think of
the joy you feel handing over your money when
you pay for an incredible bargain.

~ *D.W. Brown*

If you find a path with no obstacles,
it probably doesn't lead anywhere interesting.

~ *Frank A. Clark*

Success is the ability to go from one
failure to another with no loss of enthusiasm.

~ *Winston Churchill*

Cultivate the tree which you have found to bear fruit in
your soil. Regard not your past failures or successes.
All the past is equally a failure and a success;
it is a success in as much as it offers you the present opportunity.
~ *Henry David Thoreau*

Failures, *repeated* failures, are sign-posts on the road
to achievement. The only time you don't want to fail
is the last time you try something (and it works).
~ *Charles F. Kettering*

I have not failed 10,000 times.
I have successfully found 10,000 ways that will not work.
~ *Thomas Edison*

Don't say "Oops." Say, "Ah, interesting."
~ *Anonymous*

Like a plant that starts up in showers and sunshine
and does not know which has best helped it to grow,
it is difficult to say whether the hard things
or the pleasant things did me the most good.
~ *Lucy Larcom*

Forget mistakes. Forget failure.
Forget everything except what you're going
to do now and do it. Today is your lucky day.
~ *Will Durant*

Life is not an exact science, it is an art.
~ *Samuel Butler*

A day dawns, quite like other days;
in it a single hour comes, quite like other hours;
but in that day and in that hour
the chance of a lifetime faces us.
~ *Maltbie Babcock*

Be prepared for truth at all hours and in
the most fantastic disguises. This is the only safety.
~ *Christopher Morley*

It is not the strongest of the species that survives,
nor the most intelligent that survives.
It is the one that is most adaptable to change.
~ *Leon C. Megginson*

Luck never gives; it only lends.
~ *Swedish proverb*

Good luck is often with the man
who doesn't include it in his plans.

~ *Anonymous*

We cannot make it rain, but we can see to it
that the rain falls on prepared soil.

~ *Henri Nouwen*

What helps luck is a habit of watching for opportunities,
of having a patient but restless mind, of sacrificing
one's ease or vanity, of uniting a love of detail to foresight,
and of passing through hard times bravely and cheerfully.

~ *Charles Victor Cherbuliez*

Fortune befriends the bold.

~ *John Dryden*

Chance favors those in motion.

~ *James H. Austin*

He that would have fruit must climb the tree.

~ *Thomas Fuller*

If you can take the worst, take the risk.

~ *Anonymous*

To achieve greatness, you must be prepared
to dabble on the boundary of disaster.

~ *Henry Adams*

We are not prisoners in a foreign environment.
We have been put into life, as into the element
we are most suitable for, like fish in water.
If we understand that we must always trust in the difficult,
then what appears as the most alien of things
can become among our most intimate and beloved experiences.
Perhaps all that appears terrible to us is
in its essence something helpless that needs help from us.

~ *Rainer Maria Rilke*

To conquer without risk is to triumph without glory.

~ *Pierre Corneille*

All life is a chance. So take it!

~ *Dale Carnegie*

II.
HAPPY ACTION

☙

Success is that old ABC — ability, breaks, and courage.
~ *Charles Luckman*

When making a decision of minor importance,
I have always found it advantageous to
consider all the pros and cons. In vital matters,
however, such as the choice of a mate or a profession,
the decision should come from the unconscious,
from somewhere within ourselves.
In the important decisions of personal life,
we should be governed, I think,
by the deep inner needs of our nature.
~ *Sigmund Freud*

Inspirations never go in for long engagements;
they demand immediate marriage to action.
~ *Brendan Francis*

Don't do nothing because you can't do everything.
Do something. Do anything.
~ *Colleen Patrick-Goudreau*

That is the principal thing — not to remain with the dream,
with the intention, with the being-in-the-mood,
but always forcibly to convert it into all things.
~ *Rainer Maria Rilke*

If a man wants his dream to come true, he must wake up.
~ *Anonymous*

I have now spent fifty-five years in resolving;
having, from the earliest time almost that I can remember,
been forming plans of a better life. I have done nothing.
~ *Samuel Johnson*

Our main business is not to see what lies
dimly at a distance, but to do what lies clearly at hand.
~ *Thomas Carlyle*

The question for each man to settle
is not what he would do if he had means, time,
influence, and educational advantages,
but what he will do with the things he has.
~ *Hamilton Wright Mabie*

Optimism, unaccompanied by personal effort,
is merely a state of mind and not fruitful.
~ *Edward Curtis*

The world cares very little about what a man
or woman knows; it is what a man or woman
is able to do that counts.

~ *Booker T. Washington*

Activity in the back of a very small idea will produce
more than inactivity and the planning of a genius.

~ *James A. Worsham*

There are two words that describe every military disaster: too late.

~ *Douglas MacArthur*

Defeat is a thing of weariness, of incoherence, of boredom.

~ *Antoine de Saint-Exupéry*

The world belongs to the enthusiast who keeps cool.

~ *William McFee*

Flaming enthusiasm, backed up by
horse sense and persistence, is the quality that
most frequently makes for success.

~ *Dale Carnegie*

Make choices based on *what* gives you
a sense of fulfillment, not fear.

~ *Pauline Rose Clance*

A lively, gifted spirit, keeping as closely as possible
with a practical intention to what is nearest of all,
is the most excellent thing on earth.

~ *Johann Wolfgang von Goethe*

Apathy can be overcome by enthusiasm,
and enthusiasm can only be aroused by two things:
first, an ideal, which takes the imagination by storm,
and, second, a definite intelligible plan
for carrying that ideal out into practice.

~ *Arnold Toynbee*

If you want to build a ship, don't drum up men to
gather the wood, divide the work, and give orders.
Instead, teach them to yearn for the vast and endless sea.

~ *Antoine de Saint-Exupéry*

The secret of discipline is motivation.
When a man is sufficiently motivated,
discipline will take care of itself.

~ *Alexander Paterson*

Many persons have a wrong idea of what constitutes
true happiness. It is not attained through self-gratification,
but through fidelity to a worthy purpose.

~ *Helen Keller*

To win true peace, a man needs to feel himself directed, pardoned, and sustained by a supreme power, to feel himself in the right road, at the point where God would have him be — in order with God and the universe. This faith gives strength and calm.

~ *Henri Amiel*

This is the true joy in life, the being used for a purpose recognized by yourself as a mighty one …
the being a force of Nature instead of being a feverish selfish little clod of ailments and grievances complaining that the world will not devote itself to making you happy.

~ *George Bernard Shaw*

Don't worry about what the world needs.
Ask what makes you come alive and do that.
Because what the world needs are people who have come alive.

~ *Howard Thurman*

No man is a failure who is enjoying life.

~ *William Feather*

In all abundance there is lack.

~ *Hippocrates*

Be happy. It's one way of being wise.

~ *Colette*

Not what we have, but what we enjoy,
constitutes our abundance.

~ *John Petit-Senn*

'Tis not the meat, but 'tis the appetite
Makes eating a delight.

~ *John Suckling*

We act as though comfort and luxury
were the chief requirements of life,
when all that we need to make us happy
is something to be enthusiastic about.

~ *Charles Kingsley*

It is not our level of prosperity that
makes for happiness, but the kinship of heart
to heart and the way we look at the world.
Both attitudes lie within our power.

~ *Alexander Solzhenitsyn*

The secret of life is to have a task, something you devote your
entire life to, something you bring everything to, every minute of
the day for your whole life. And the most important thing is —
it must be something you cannot possibly do!

~ *Henry Moore*

I arise in the morning torn between a desire to improve
(or save) the world and a desire to enjoy (or savor) the world.
This makes it hard to plan the day.

~ *Elwyn Brooks White*

There are three ingredients in the good life:
learning, earning, and yearning.

~ *Christopher Morley*

Most men pursue pleasure with such breathless haste
that they hurry past it.

~ *Søren Kierkegaard*

If we only wanted to be happy it would be easy; but we want
to be happier than other people, which is almost always difficult,
since we think them happier than they are.

~ *Charles de Montesquieu*

Condition, circumstance, is not the thing;
Bliss is the same in peasant or in king.

~ Alexander Pope

Happiness is an imaginary condition, formerly attributed
by the living to the dead, now usually attributed by adults
to children, and by children to adults.

~ Thomas Szasz

Before we set our hearts too much upon anything,
let us examine how happy those are who already possess it.

~ François de La Rochefoucauld

We spend our time searching for security
and hate it when we get it.

~ John Steinbeck

Possessions are generally diminished by possession.

~ Friedrich Nietzsche

The wisdom of life consists in the elimination of non-essentials.

~ Lin Yutang

Think contentment the greatest wealth.

~ George Shelley

Are you not ashamed of heaping up the greatest
amount of money and honor and reputation,
and caring so little about wisdom and truth and
the greatest improvement of the soul?

~ *Socrates*

It is very wrong for people to feel deeply sad
when they lose some money, yet when
they waste the precious moments of their lives
they do not have the slightest feeling of repentance.

~ *The Dalai Lama*

There was a preacher who would pray with great earnestness
for thieves and swindlers, and he was asked, "Why do you
pray for these bad people?" He responded by saying,
"Because I am grateful to them. When they take from me the
things they desire, I am reminded that what they want is not
what I want. In this way, they keep me on my path. There
can be more danger from those who offer me the kinds of
comforts that keep me from true contentment.
Sometimes friends are enemies and enemies are friends.

~ *Rumi*

The secret of happiness is to admire without desiring.

~ *F. H. Bradley*

Or have you only comfort, and the lust for comfort,
that stealthy thing that enters the house a guest,
and then becomes a host, and then a master?
~ *Kahlil Gibran*

I can complain because rose bushes have thorns,
or rejoice that thorn bushes have roses.
~ *J. Kenfield Morley*

We either make ourselves miserable,
or we make ourselves strong.
The amount of work is the same.
~ *Carlos Castaneda*

There is nothing either good or bad,
but thinking makes it so.
~ *William Shakespeare*, Hamlet

We are not miserable without feeling it.
A ruined house is not miserable.
~ *Blaise Pascal*

Do not value money for any more nor any less
than its worth; it is a good servant but a bad master.
~ *Alexandre Dumas fils*, Camille

Happiness comes out of the capacity to feel deeply,
to enjoy simply, to think freely, to risk life, to be needed.

~ *Storm Jameson*

If an Arab in the desert were suddenly to discover a spring
in his tent, and so would always be able to have water in
abundance, how fortunate he would consider himself; so too,
when a man who is always turned toward the outside, thinking
that his happiness lies outside himself, finally turns inward
and discovers that the source is within.

~ *Søren Kierkegaard*

The lesson which life repeats and constantly enforces is
"Look under your foot." You are always nearer the
divine and the true sources of your power than you think.
The lure of the distant and the difficult is deceptive.
The great opportunity is where you are. Do not despise
your own place and hour. Every place is under the stars,
every place is the center of the world.

~ *John Burroughs*

The really happy man is the one who can
enjoy the scenery when he has to take a detour.

~ *Anonymous*

And so the most insignificant present
has over the most significant past the advantage of reality.
~ *Arthur Schopenhauer*

Dwell as near as possible to the channel in which your life flows.
~ *Henry David Thoreau*

Live as if you were to die tomorrow.
Learn as if you were to live forever.
~ *Mahatma Gandhi*

When I am anxious it is because I am living in the future.
When I am depressed it is because I am living in the past.
~ *Anonymous*

He who postpones the hour of living
rightly is like the fool who waits
for the river to run out before he crosses.
~ *Horace*

Not every end is a goal. The end of a melody is not
its goal; but nonetheless, if the melody had not
reached its end it would not have reached its goal either.
~ *Friedrich Nietzsche*

With everything that we do, we desire more or less the end;
we are impatient to be done with it and glad
when it is finished. It is only the end in general, the end of all
ends, that we wish, as a rule, to put off as long as possible.

~ *Arthur Schopenhauer*

Time is a great teacher, but unfortunately it kills all its pupils.

~ *Hector Berlioz*

O my soul, do not aspire to immortal life,
but exhaust the limits of the possible.

~ *Pindar*

Don't cry because it's over, smile because it happened.

~ *Theodore Geisel, a.k.a. "Dr. Seuss"*

No longer forward nor behind
I look in hope or fear;
But, grateful, take the good I find,
The best of now and here.

~ *John Greenleaf Whittier*

III.
BRAVE COMMITMENT

A little boy was asked how he learned to skate.
"By getting up every time I fell down," he answered.
~ *David Seabury*

Fall seven times, stand up eight.
~ *Japanese proverb*

We're still not where we're going
but we're still not where we were.
~ *Natasha Jasefowitz*

Now if you are going to win any battle you have to do
one thing. You have to make the mind run the body.
Never let the body tell the mind what to do. The body
will always give up. It is always tired morning, noon, and night.
But the body is never tired if the mind is not tired.... You've
always got to make the mind take over and keep going.
~ *George S. Patton*

Don't watch the clock; do what it does. Don't stop.
~ *Sam Levenson*

He who limps is still walking.

~ *Stanislaw J. Lec*

To be happy, drop the words "if only"
and substitute instead the words "next time."

~ *Smiley Blanton*

When you're a professional, you come back
no matter what happened the day before.

~ *Billy Martin*

A professional is someone who can do his best work
when he doesn't feel like it.

~ *Alistair Cooke*

It's a little like wrestling a gorilla. You don't quit
when you're tired — you quit when the gorilla is tired.

~ *Robert Strauss*

I never lost a game; sometimes I just ran out of time.

~ *Bobby Layne*

They were never defeated; they were only killed.

~ *French Foreign Legion expression*

The question is not whether you're frightened or not,
but whether you or your fear is in control.
If you say, "I won't be frightened," and then experience fear,
most likely you'll succumb to it, because you're paying
attention to it. The correct thing to tell yourself is,
"If I do get frightened, I will stay in command."

~ *Herbert Fensterheim*

Courage is not the absence of fear, but rather
the judgment that something is more important than fear.

~ *Ambrose Redman*

Fear is like fire:
if controlled, it will help you; if uncontrolled,
it will rise up and destroy you.

~ *John F. Milburn*

Cowardice … is almost always simply a lack
of ability to suspend the functioning of the imagination.

~ *Ernest Hemingway*

Fear cannot be without hope, nor hope without fear.

~ *Baruch Spinoza*

Fear is faith that it won't work out.

~ *Mary Tricky*

Anxiety is nothing but repeatedly
re-experiencing failure in advance.

~ *Anonymous*

In times of danger it is proper to be alarmed
until danger be near at hand; but when we perceive that danger
is near, we should oppose it as if we were not afraid.

~ *Hitopadesa*

When danger approaches, sing to it.

~ *Arabian proverb*

A person in danger should not try to escape at one stroke.
He should first calmly hold his own, then be satisfied
with small gains, which will come by creative adaptations.

~ *I Ching*

Are you as frightened as you've ever been or could be? No?
Then it's not that bad. If you are at this moment as afraid
as you ever could be — good, then the worst is over.

~ *Jean Anouilh*, The Lark

Courage comes and goes. Hold on for the next supply.

~ *Thomas Merton*

Things done well
And with a care exempt themselves from fear.
~ *William Shakespeare,* Henry VIII

It is only when I dally with what I am about,
look back, and aside, instead of keeping my eyes straight forward,
that I feel these cold sinkings of the heart.
~ *Sir Walter Scott*

Obstacles are those frightful things
you see when you take your eyes off the goal.
~ *Hannah More*

Every problem contains within itself the seeds of its own solution.
~ *Stanley Arnold*

The most drastic and usually
the most effective remedy for fear is direct action.
~ *William Burnham*

Action is the antidote to despair.
~ *Joan Baez*

Danger itself is usually the best remedy for danger.
~ *Anonymous*

It doesn't work to leap a twenty-foot chasm
in two ten-foot jumps.

~ *American proverb*

The first idea that the child must acquire, in order to be actively
disciplined, is that of the difference between good and evil;
and the task of the educator lies in seeing that the child does not
confound good with immobility, and evil with activity.

~ *Maria Montessori*

Facing it, always facing it, that's the way to get through.
Face it!

~ *Joseph Conrad*

Do what you can, with what you have, where you are.

~ *Theodore Roosevelt*

Do not let what you cannot do interfere with what you can do.

~ *John Wooden*

We must look for the opportunity in every
difficulty instead of being paralyzed at the
thought of the difficulty in every opportunity.

~ *Walter E. Cole*

Opportunity's favorite disguise is trouble.
~ *Frank Tyger*

Strength is a matter of the made-up mind.
~ *John Beecher*

Pray not for a lighter burden, but for broader shoulders.
~ *Jewish prayer*

Prudence which degenerates into timidity
is very seldom the path to safety.
~ *Viscount Cecil*

Why should a man fear, since chance is all in all for him,
and he can clearly fore-know nothing?
Best to live lightly as one can, unthinking.
~ *Sophocles*, Oedipus

It is the business of the future to be dangerous.
~ *Alfred North Whitehead*

The most precious thing in life is its uncertainty.
~ *Yoshida Kenko*

The world is quite right. It does not have to be consistent.
~ *Charlotte Perkins Gilman*

The man who insists upon seeing with
perfect clearness before he decides, never decides.
~ *Henri Frédéric Amiel*

I have made decisions that turned out to be wrong,
and went back and did it another way, and still took less time
than many who procrastinated over the original decision.
~ *Jerry Gillies*

While one person hesitates because he feels inferior,
the other is busy making mistakes and becoming superior.
~ *Henry Link*

In not making the decision, you've made one.
Not doing something is the same as doing it.
~ *Ivan Bloch*

You will be more disappointed by the things you didn't do than
by the things you did. So throw off the bowlines.
Sail away from the safe harbor. Catch the trade winds in your
sails. Explore. Dream. Discover.
~ *Mark Twain*

There is a time for departure
even when there's no certain place to go.
~ *Tennessee Williams*, Camino Real

Look on every exit being an entrance somewhere else.
~ *Tom Stoppard*, Rosencrantz and Guildenstern are Dead

Life is not long, and too much of it should not
be spent in idle deliberation how it shall be spent.
~ *Samuel Johnson*

He who deliberates before taking a step
will spend his entire life on one leg.
~ *Chinese proverb*

The moment one definitely commits oneself,
then providence moves too. A whole stream of events
issues from the decision, raising in one's favor
all manner of unforeseen incidents, meetings and
material assistance, which no man could have dreamt
would have come his way.
~ *W. H. Murray*

You can have anything you want if you want it desperately enough. You must want it with an exuberance that erupts through the skin and joins the energy that created the world.

~ *Sheila Graham*

You must bring every particle of your energy, unanswerable resolution, your best efforts, your persistent industry to your task or the best will not come out of you. You must back up your ambition by your whole nature, by unbounded enthusiasm and a determination to win which knows no failure.

~ *Orison Swett Marden*

It is only when you despair of all ordinary means, it is only when you convince it that it must help you or you perish, that the seed of life in you bestirs itself to provide a new resource.

~ *Robert Collier*

If you take any activity, any art, any discipline, any skill, take it and push it as far as it will go ... push it to the wildest edge of edges, then you force it into the realm of magic.

~ *Tom Robbins*, Even Cowgirls Get The Blues

Courage doesn't always roar. Sometimes courage is the little voice at the end of the day that says I'll try again tomorrow.

~ *Mary Anne Radmacher*

The world has no room for cowards.
We must all be ready somehow to toil, to suffer, to die.
And yours is not the less noble because no drum beats
before you, when you go out into your daily battlefields;
and no crowds shout about your coming,
when you return from your daily victory or defeat.

~ Robert Louis Stevenson

Whatever course you decide upon, there is always
someone to tell you that you are wrong. There are always
difficulties arising which tempt you to believe that
your critics are right. To map out a course of action and
follow it to an end requires courage.

~ Ralph Waldo Emerson

The person who says it cannot be done
should not interrupt the person who is doing it.

~ Chinese proverb

The man who can't dance thinks the band is no good.

~ Polish proverb

Never tell a young person that anything cannot be done.
God may have been waiting centuries for someone
ignorant enough of the impossible to do that very thing.

~ John Andrew Holmes

Keep away from people who try to belittle your ambitions.
Small people always do that, but the really great make you feel
that you, too, can become great.

~ *Mark Twain*

It is not the critic who counts; not the man who points out
how the strong man stumbles or where the doer of deeds could
have done them better. The credit belongs to the man who
is actually in the arena, whose face is marred by dust and sweat
and blood; who strives valiantly; who errs, and comes short
again and again, because there is no effort without error and
shortcoming; but who does actually strive to do the deeds;
who knows the great enthusiasms, the great devotions; who
spends himself in a worthy cause; who at the best knows in the
end the triumph of high achievement, and who at the worst, if
he fails, at least fails while daring greatly.

~ *Teddy Roosevelt*

Knock the "t" off the "can't."

~ *George Reeves*

You do what you can for as long as you can,
and when you finally can't, you do the next best thing.
You back up but you don't give up.

~ *Chuck Yeager*

When you come to the end of your rope, tie a knot and hang on.
~ *Franklin D. Roosevelt*

The greatest test of courage on the earth
is to bear defeat without losing heart.
~ *Robert G. Ingersoll*

The test of a vocation is the love of the drudgery it involves.
~ *Logan Pearsall Smith*

No one ever did anything worth doing unless he was prepared
to go on with it long after it became something of a bore.
~ *Douglas V. Steere*

The price one pays for pursuing any profession,
or calling, is an intimate knowledge of its ugly side.
~ *James Baldwin*

If you live in the river, make friends with the crocodile.
~ *Indian proverb (Punjabi)*

The height of your accomplishments
will equal the depth of your convictions.
~ *William F. Scolavino*

Courage, in its final analysis, is nothing but an
affirmative answer to the shocks of existence.

~ *Kurt Goldstein*

The big thing is to combine punctuality, efficiency,
good nature, obedience, intelligence, and concentration
with an unawareness of what is going to happen next,
thus keeping yourself available for excitement.

~ *John Gielgud*

Dare to be naive.

~ *Buckminster Fuller*

One must have chaos in one to give birth to a dancing star.

~ *Friedrich Nietzsche*

The most powerful weapon on earth is the human soul on fire.

~ *Ferdinand Foch*

I will find a way, or make one.

~ *Robert Sidney*

There are always two paths to take: one back towards the
comfort and security of death, the other forward to nowhere.

~ *Henry Miller*, The Colossus of Maroussi

The passions are the winds that fill the sails of the vessel,
and sink it at times; but without them it would be
impossible to make way.... Everything is dangerous
here below, but everything is necessary.

~ *Voltaire*

The desire for safety stands against every great and noble enterprise.

~ *Cornelius Tacitus*

Every good and excellent thing in the world stands moment by
moment on the razor-edge of danger and must be fought for.

~ *Thornton Wilder*, The Skin of Our Teeth

Necessity has no law.

~ *St. Augustine*

Victory is a thing of the will.

~ *Ferdinand Foch*

Victory belongs to the most persevering.

~ *Napoleon Bonaparte*

It doesn't matter how slowly you go, as long as you do not stop.

~ *Confucius*

Do what thou wilt.

~ *François Rabelais*

Live to the point of tears.

~ *Albert Camus*

We are here to laugh at the odds and live our lives
so well that Death will tremble to take us.

~ *Charles Bukowski*

Come follow me and let the world babble.

~ *Dante Alighieri*, The Divine Comedy

IV.

A Best Self

Be not the slave of words.

~ *Thomas Carlyle*

We think and name in one world,
we live and feel in another.

~ *Marcel Proust*, The Guermantes Way

Every definition is dangerous.

~ *Desiderius Erasmus*

To understand is almost the opposite of existing.

~ *George Poulet*

The best answers are those that destroy the questions.

~ *Susan Sontag*

In each of us there is another whom we do not know.
He speaks to us in dreams and tells us how differently he sees us from
the way we see ourselves. To me dreams are a part of nature, which
harbors no intent to deceive, but expresses something as best it can.

~ *Carl Jung*

In all of us, even in good men, there is
a lawless wild-beast nature, which peers out in sleep.

~ *Plato*

The natural inheritance of everyone who is capable of
spiritual life is an unsubdued forest where the wolf howls
and the obscene bird of night chatters.

~ *Henry James, Sr.*

He is born without his own consent ... his ideas
come to him involuntarily; his habits are in the power
of those who cause him to contract them;
he is unceasingly modified by causes, whether visible
or concealed, over which he has no control, which
necessarily regulate his mode of existence,
give the hue to his way of thinking, and determine
his manner of acting.... Nevertheless, in spite of
the shackles by which he is bound, it is pretended he
is a free agent, or that independent of the causes by
which he is moved, he determines his own will,
and regulates his own condition.

~ *Paul-Henri Thiry*

The more conscious you become, the more unconscious
you realize you are. You don't stop. There is no stopping place.
There is an openness that is part of a new style of thinking.

~ *Patricia Sun*

The man who stands still in the midst of the struggle and says,
"I have it," merely shows by so doing that he has just lost it.

~ *Henrik Ibsen*

All supreme questions, all ultimate problems of value
are beyond human reason.

~ *Friedrich Nietzsche*

The intelligent man who is proud of his intelligence
is like a condemned man who is proud of his large cell.

~ Simone Weil

We know too much and feel too little.

~ Bertrand Russell

Knowledge shrinks as wisdom grows,
for details are swallowed up in principles.

~ Alfred Lord Whitehead

With wisdom grows doubt.

~ Johann Wolfgang von Goethe

Doubt is not a pleasant condition, but certainty is absurd.

~ Voltaire

The plain fact is that there are no conclusions.

~ James Jeans

Something unknown is doing we don't know what.

~ Arthur Eddington

The larger the island of knowledge,
the longer the shoreline of wonder.

~ *Ralph W. Sockman*

I used to think that the human brain was the most wonderful
organ in my body. Then I realized who was telling me this.

~ *Emo Phillips*

Be patient toward all that is unsolved in your heart
and try to love the questions themselves.

~ *Rainer Maria Rilke*

Seek not thou to find
The sacred counsels of almighty mind;
Involv'd in darkness lies the great decree,
Nor can the depths of fate be pierc'd by thee.

~ *Homer*, The Iliad

Two people were looking out over the ocean and one said:
"Look at all that water."
The other replied: "Yeah. And that's just the top of it."

~ *Anonymous*

Let mystery have its place in you; do not be always
turning up your whole soil with the ploughshare
of self-examination, but leave a little fallow corner
in your heart ready for any seed the winds may bring,
and reserve a nook of shadow for the passing bird.

~ *Henri Amiel*

[The artist] opens himself to *all* influences —
everything nourishes him. Everything is gravy to him,
including what he does *not* understand —
particularly what he does *not* understand.

~ *Henry Miller*

There are two worlds. One is fake, the other keeps moving
its location. As soon as you know anything, you are in fake world
where everything is dead. The other world has no name,
no definite shape, no fixed rules, and you're stepping over corpses
and around broken glass and garbage all the time.
And that's where you'll find God.

~ *John Patrick Shanley*

Fill your bowl to the brim and it will spill.
Keep sharpening your knife and it will blunt.

~ *Lao Tzu*

The great man is he who does not lose his child-heart.

~ *Mencius*

To be surprised, to wonder, is to begin to understand.

~ *José Ortega y Gasset*

Live your own life, for you will surely die your own death.

~ *Latin proverb*

Our concern must be to *live* while we're alive —
to release our inner selves from the spiritual death that
comes with living behind a facade designed to conform
to external definitions of who and what we are.

~ *Elizabeth Kubler-Ross*

One's real life is so often the life that one does not lead.

~ *Oscar Wilde*

So much must I live for others,
that almost I am a stranger to myself.

~ *Innocent III*

Nobody can be exactly like me.
Sometimes even I have trouble doing it.

~ *Tallulah Bankhead*

If I am transparent enough to myself, then I can become
less afraid of those hidden selves that my transparency
may reveal to others. If I reveal myself without worrying about
how others will respond, then some will care, though
others may not. But who can love me, if no one knows me?
I must risk it, or live alone.

~ *Sheldon Kopp*

All paths lead to the same goal: to convey to others what we are.

~ *Pablo Neruda*

There is only one success —
to be able to spend your life in your own way.

~ *Christopher Morley*

I should love to satisfy all, if I possibly can; but in trying
to satisfy all, I may be able to satisfy none ... the
best course is to satisfy one's own conscience and leave
the world to form its own judgment, favorable or otherwise.

~ *Mahatma Gandhi*

Be who you are and say what you feel,
because those who mind don't matter
and those who matter don't mind.

~ *Theodore Geisel, a.k.a. "Dr. Seuss"*

No one can make you feel inferior without your consent.

~ *Eleanor Roosevelt*

ॐ

Nothing has a stronger influence psychologically on
their environment, and especially on their children,
than the unlived life of the parents.

~ *Carl Jung*

Those who in their youth did not live in self-harmony,
and who did not gain the true treasures of life,
are later like long-legged old herons standing sadly by
a lake without fish.

~ *The Dhammapada*

Don't worry that [your children] never listen to you;
worry that they are always watching you.

~ *Robert Fulghum*

God help all children as they move into a time of life they
don't understand and must struggle through the precepts
picked from the garbage cans of older people, clinging to odds
and ends that will mess them up for all time, or hating the
trash so much they'll waste their future on the hatred.

~ *Lillian Hellman*

What you have become is the price
you paid to get what you used to want.

~ *Mignon McLaughlin*

Without our familiar props, we are faced with just ourselves,
a person who we do not know, an unnerving stranger
with whom we have been living all the time but we never really
wanted to meet. Isn't that why we have tried to fill every
moment of time with noise and activity, however boring or trivial,
to ensure that we are never left in silence with this stranger on our own?

~ *Sogyal Rinpoche*

Whatever is rejected from the self, appears in the world as an event.

~ *Carl Jung*

The individual has always had to struggle to keep from being
overwhelmed by the tribe. If you try it, you will be lonely often,
and sometimes frightened. But no price is too high to pay
for the privilege of owning yourself.

~ *Friedrich Nietzsche*

The privilege of a lifetime is being who you are.

~ *Joseph Campbell*

To be nobody-but-yourself — in a world which is doing its best,
night and day, to make you everybody else —
means to fight the hardest battle which any human being can fight;
and never stop fighting.

~ *e.e. cummings*

Sometimes snakes can't slough. They can't burst their old skin.
Then they go sick and die inside the old skin, and nobody ever
sees the new pattern. It needs a real desperate recklessness to burst
your old skin at last. You simply don't care what happens to you,
if you rip yourself in two, so long as you do get out.

~ *James Fenimore Cooper*

To know what you prefer instead of humbly saying
Amen to what the world tells you you ought to prefer,
is to have kept your soul alive.

~ *Robert Louis Stevenson*

Is life not a hundred times too short for us to stifle ourselves?

~ *Friedrich Nietzsche*

So, throughout life, our worst weaknesses and meannesses are
usually committed for the sake of the people whom we most despise.

~ *Charles Dickens*, Great Expectations

In the presence of some people we inevitably depart
from ourselves: we are inaccurate, we say things we do not feel,
and talk nonsense. When we get home we are conscious that we
have made fools of ourselves. Never go near these people.

~ *François de La Rochefoucauld*

Nothing so much prevents our being natural
as the desire of appearing so.

~ *D. H. Lawrence*

Because you're not what I would have you be
I blind myself to who, in truth, you are.

~ *Madeline L'Engle*

Man is what he believes.

~ *Anton Chekhov*

For what we wish, that we readily believe.

~ *Demosthenes*

Faced with the choice between changing one's
mind and proving that there is no need to do so,
almost everyone gets busy on the proof.

~ *John Kenneth Galbraith*

You can't wake a person who is pretending to be asleep.
~ *Navajo proverb*

Nothing is more desirable than to be released from an affliction,
but nothing is more frightening than to be divested of a crutch.
~ *James Baldwin*

We do not err because truth is difficult to see. It is visible at a
glance. We err because this is more comfortable.
~ *Alexander Solzhenitsyn*

Most of the time we are only partially alive.
Most of our faculties go on sleeping because they rely
on habit which can function without them.
~ *Marcel Proust*, In Search of Lost Time

With us in the West, wakefulness, for some mysterious reason,
comes and goes. Our understanding fires up briefly
but invariably fades again. Sometimes I suspect that I am myself
under a frightful hypnotic influence — I do and do not know
the evils of our times.... Then I begin against reason to suspect
the influence of a diffusing power — a demonic will that opposes
our understanding: I am forced to consider whether Western
Europe and the United States may not be under the influence of a
great evil, whether we do not go about "lightly chloroformed."
~ *Saul Bellow*

Man cannot persist long in a conscious state,
he must throw himself back into the unconscious,
for his root lives there
~ *Johann Wolfgang von Goethe*

If one can actually revert to the truth, then a great deal
of one's suffering can be erased — because a
great deal of one's suffering is based on sheer lies.
~ *R. D. Laing*

Real difficulties can be overcome; it is only
the imaginary ones that are unconquerable.
~ *Theodore Vail*

Because our goals are not lofty, but illusory,
our problems are not difficult, but nonsensical.
~ *Ludwig Wittgenstein*

The most useful piece of learning for the uses
of life is to unlearn what is untrue.
~ *Antisthenes*

How many legs does a dog have if you call the tail a leg?
Four. Calling a tail a leg doesn't make it a leg.
~ *Abraham Lincoln*

People have many illusions that block them from acting in their own best interest. In dealing with the present problems of life, we must first be able to see the reality of our lives.

~ *Jonas Salk*

To avoid disillusionment with human nature,
we must first give up our illusions about it.

~ *Abraham Maslow*

The keenest sorrow is to recognize ourselves
as the sole cause of all our adversities.

~ *Sophocles*, Antigone

I know that most men ... can seldom discern even the simplest and most obvious truth if it be such as obliges them to admit the falsity of conclusions they have formed, perhaps with much difficulty — conclusions of which they are proud, which they have taught to others, and on which they have built their lives.

~ *Leo Tolstoy*

When you plant lettuce, if it does not grow well,
you don't blame the lettuce. You look into the reasons it is
not doing well. It may need fertilizer, or more water,
or less sun. You never blame the lettuce.

~ *Thich Nhat Hanh*

Make no excuses. You don't have time, because if you use your
energy that way, you won't have any energy to deal with what you need
to deal with, which is overcoming obstacles and obtaining goals.
~ *Frances Williams*

The majority of men are subjective towards themselves
and objective towards all others, terribly objective sometimes —
but the real task is in fact to be objective
towards oneself and subjective towards all others.
~ *Søren Kierkegaard*

The truth will set you free. But before it does, it will make you angry.
~ *Jerry Joiner*

I'm always ready to learn, even though I do not always like being taught.
~ *Winston Churchill*

Everyone is a prisoner of his own experiences.
No one can eliminate prejudices — just recognize them.
~ *Edward R. Murrow*

Alas, I know if I ever became truly humble, I would be proud of it.
~ *Benjamin Franklin*

If you think you are not conceited, it means you are very conceited indeed.
~ *C. S. Lewis*

I don't want the cheese anymore, I just want out of the trap.

~ *Spanish proverb*

What is a man's first duty? To be himself.

~ *Henrik Ibsen*, Peer Gynt

What is the freedom of the most free? To act rightly!

~ *Johann Wolfgang von Goethe*

I ought never to act except in such a way that I can also will that my maxim should become a universal law.

~ *Immanuel Kant*

You have to be true to yourself, but you have to be true to your best self, not to the self that secretly thinks you are better than other people.

~ *Stephen Gaskin*

Freedom means choosing your burden.

~ *Hephzibah Menuhin*

Forge your tongue on the anvil of truth.

~ *Pindar*

One has not the right to betray even a traitor.
Traitors must be fought, not betrayed.
~ *Charles Pierre Péguy*

Two things fill the mind with ever new and increasing admiration
and awe, the more often and steadily reflection is occupied
with them: *the starry heaven above me and the moral law within me.*
~ *Immanuel Kant*

What is moral is what you feel good after
and what is immoral is what you feel bad after.
~ *Ernest Hemingway*

I speak truth, not so much as I would, but as much as I dare,
and I dare a little the more, as I grow older.
~ *Michel de Montaigne*

The truth is always somewhere else.
~ *Peter Brook*

Everything possible to be believed is an image of truth.
~ *William Blake*

Seek simplicity and distrust it.
~ *Alfred Lord Whitehead*

I am a man: nothing human is alien to me.

~ *Terence*

Treat others as you want them to treat you.

~ *Anonymous*

Never undertake anything for which you wouldn't have
the courage to ask the blessings of heaven.

~ *Georg Christoph Lichtenberg*

If you compromise with your own conscience, it will not be long
before you will have no conscience because your conscience
will fail to guide you, just as an alarm clock will fail to awaken
you if you do not heed it.

~ *Napoleon Hill*

We ought always to employ our vigilance, with most attention, on
that enemy from which there is the greatest danger, and to stray,
if we must stray, towards those parts from whence we may quickly
and easily return.

~ *Samuel Johnson*

Be at war with your vices.

~ *Benjamin Franklin*

Always put off until tomorrow what you shouldn't do at all.

~ *Anonymous*

If you aren't willing to discipline yourself,
the physical universe will do it for you.

~ *Leonard Orr*

In a fight between you and the world, bet on the world.

~ *Franz Kafka*

Ruled by the rudder or ruled by the rock.

~ *Cornish proverb*

Seek freedom and become captive of your desires.
Seek discipline and find your liberty.

~ *Frank Herbert*, Chapterhouse: Dune

Human life is meant for a little austerity. We have to purify
our existence; that is the mission of human life ... because
then you will get spiritual realization, the unlimited, endless
pleasure and happiness. That is real pleasure, real happiness.

~ *A. C. Bhaktivedanta*

If it's bad for you, don't do it. If it's good for you, do it.

~ *Anonymous*

Physiologists should think twice before positioning the drive for
self-preservation as the cardinal drive of an organic being.
Above all, a living thing wants to discharge its strength — life
itself is will to power — self-preservation is only one of the
indirect and most frequent consequences of this.

~ *Friedrich Nietzsche*

The love of glory, the fear of disgrace, the incentive to succeed,
the desire to live in comfort, and the instinct to humiliate others
are often the cause of that courage so renowned among men.

~ *François de La Rochefoucauld*

Life as we find it is too hard for us; it entails too much pain,
too many disappointments, impossible tasks. We cannot
do without palliative remedies.... There are perhaps three of
these means: powerful diversions of interest, which lead us
to care little about our misery; substitutive gratification, which
lessen it; and intoxicating substances, which make us insensitive
to it. Something of this kind is indispensable.

~ *Sigmund Freud*

If each of us were to confess his most secret desire,
the one that inspires all his plans, all his actions,
he would say: "I want to be praised."

~ *E. M. Cioran*

The applause of a single human being is of great consequence.

~ *Samuel Johnson*

I never met a man so mean that
I was not willing he should admire me.

~ *Edgar Watson Howe*

No siren did ever so charm the ear of the listener
as the listening ear has charmed the soul of the siren.

~ *Henry Taylor*

Charm is that quality in others
that makes us more satisfied with ourselves.

~ *Henri-Frédéric Amiel*

Sometimes we deny being worthy of praise,
hoping to generate an argument we would be pleased to lose.

~ *Cullen Hightower*

When people do not respect us we are sharply offended;
yet deep down in his private heart no man much respects himself.

~ *Mark Twain*, Pudd'nhead Wilson's New Calendar

We judge ourselves by what we feel capable of doing,
while others judge us by what we have already done.

~ *Henry Wadsworth Longfellow*

The deepest principle of Human Nature
is the craving to be appreciated.

~ *William James*

The anxiety to be admired is loveless passion, ever strongest
with regard to those by whom we are least known and
least cared for, loud on the hustings, gay in the ball-room,
mute and sullen at the family fireside.

~ *Samuel Taylor Coleridge*

Popularity? It is glory's small change.

~ *Victor Hugo*

Do not trust the cheering, for those persons would shout
as much if you and I were going to be hanged.

~ *Oliver Cromwell*

In great matters people show themselves as they
wish to be seen; in small matters, as they are.

~ *Gamaliel Bradford*

Never underestimate the effectiveness of a straight cash bribe.
~ *Claude Cockburn*

We confess our faults in the plural,
and deny them in the singular.
~ *Richard Fulke Greville*

When we ask for advice,
we are usually looking for an accomplice.
~ *Marquis de La Grange*

Whoever gossips to you will gossip about you.
~ *Spanish proverb*

No one who deserves confidence ever solicits it.
~ *John Churton Collins*

Believe those who are seeking the truth. Doubt those who find it.
~ *André Gide*

Some are contented to wear the mask of foolishness in order
to carry on their vicious schemes; and not a few are willing
to shelter their folly behind the respectability of downright vice.
~ *John Stuart Mill*

Many people feel "guilty" about things they
shouldn't feel guilty about, in order to shut out feelings
of guilt about things they should feel guilty about.

~ *Sydney J. Harris*

Beggars do not envy millionaires, though of course
they will envy other beggars who are more successful.

~ *Bertrand Russell*

[Money] cuts us off from life, from vitality, from the alive sun
and the alive earth, as *nothing* can. Nothing, not even the
most fanatical dogmas of an iron-bound religion, can insulate us
from the inrush of life and inspiration, as money can.

~ *D. H. Lawrence*

They are not beautiful: they are only decorated. They are not
clean: they are only shaved and starched. They are not dignified:
they are only fashionably dressed.... They are not artistic: they
are only lascivious. They are not prosperous: they are only
rich ... liars every one of them, to the very backbone of their souls.

~ *George Bernard Shaw*, Man and Superman

Is it progress if a cannibal uses knife and fork?

~ *Stanislaw Jerzy Lec*

I was part of that strange race of people aptly described
as spending their lives doing things they detest to
make money they don't want to buy things they don't
need to impress people they dislike.

~ *Emile Henry Gauvreau*

Do not confuse your vested interests with ethics.
Do not identify the enemies of your privilege with
the enemies of humanity.

~ *Max Lerner*

Like power in any shape, a full stomach always holds
a dose of insolence, and the dose expresses itself
first of all in the well-fed lecturing the starving.

~ *Anton Chekhov*

Force is as pitiless to the man who possesses it,
or thinks he does, as it is to its victims;
the second it crushes, the first it intoxicates.
The truth is, nobody really possesses it.

~ *Simone Weil*

Distrust all in whom the impulse to punish is powerful.

~ *Friedrich Nietzsche*

Where's evil? It's that large part of every man that wants to
hate without limit, that wants to hate with God on its side.

~ *Kurt Vonnegut*, Mother Night

Evil when we are in its power is not
felt as evil but as a necessity, or even a duty.

~ *Simone Weil*

In my most evil moments I was convinced that I was doing good,
and I was well supplied with systematic arguments.... The line
separating good and evil passes not through states, nor between
classes, nor between political parties either — but right through
every human heart, and through all human hearts.

~ *Alexander Solzhenitsyn*

There is the evil of the psychopath, but, apart from its chilling
meanness, this is not so different from the bite of an unfeeling
shark. Darker evil is in an act of willful insensitivity committed by
someone who in their heart knows better.

~ *D.W. Brown*

Contempt is the weapon of the weak and a
defense against one's own despised and unwanted feelings.

~ *Alice Miller*

You can easily judge the character of a man
by how he treats those who can do nothing for him.

~ *Anonymous*

Rudeness is the weak man's imitation of strength.

~ *Eric Hoffer*

The test of good manners is to be able
to put up pleasantly with bad ones.

~ *Wendell Willkie*

The best way to knock the chip off someone's shoulder
is to pat him on the back.

~ *Anonymous*

If you hate a person, you hate something in
him that is part of yourself. What isn't part of
ourselves doesn't disturb us.

~ *Hermann Hesse*, Demian

It is hard to believe that a man is telling the truth
when you know that you would lie if you were in his place.

~ *H. L. Mencken*

A man does not look behind the door
unless he has stood there himself.

~ *Henri Du Bois*

Perhaps, there is not a more effectual key to the discovery of
hypocrisy than a censorious temper. The man possessed of real
virtue knows the difficulty of attaining it; and is, of course, more
inclined to pity others, who happen to fail in the pursuit.

~ *William Shenstone*

He may only chastise who loves.

~ *Rabindranath Tagore*

A very popular error: having the courage
of one's convictions; rather it is a matter of having
the courage for an *attack* on one's convictions!

~ *Friedrich Nietzsche*

It takes courage to stand up and speak;
it also takes courage to sit down and listen.

~ *Winston Churchill*

When the fox preaches, look to your geese.

~ *German proverb*

If your morals make you dreary, depend upon it they are wrong.
I do not say "give them up," for they may be all you have;
but conceal them like a vice,
lest they should spoil the lives of better and simpler people.

~ *Robert Lewis Stevenson*

You can straighten a worm, but the crook is in him and only waiting.

~ *Mark Twain*

We ought to see far enough into a hypocrite to see even his sincerity.

~ *G. K. Chesterton*

The most exhausting thing in life is being insincere.

~ *Anne Morrow Lindberg*

It is a secret known but to few, yet of no small use in
the conduct of life, that when you fall into a man's conversation,
the first thing you should consider is, whether he has a greater
inclination to hear you, or that you should hear him.

~ *Sir Richard Steele*

We all have the strength enough to endure the misfortunes of others.

~ *François de La Rochefoucauld*

Everything is funny as long as it's happening to someone else.

~ *Will Rogers*

We like torturing people without getting
really into trouble by killing them.

~ *Marcel Proust*

There is something in the misfortunes of
our best friends which does not wholly displease us.

~ *François de La Rochefoucauld*

My friends tell me I have an intimacy problem.
But they don't really know me.

~ *Garry Shandling*

Everything is everywhere. There are tragic elements in
superficial things and trivial in the tragic. There is something
suffocatingly sinister in what we call pleasure.

~ *Hugo Von Hofmannsthal*

An overdose of an antidote becomes a poison in itself.

~ *William Irwin Thompson*

Good swimmers are oftenest drowned.

~ *Thomas Fuller*

Place a guard over your strong points! Thrift may run
into stinginess, generosity into wastefulness or laxness.
Gentleness may become faint-heartedness, tact become insincerity,
power become oppression. Character needs sentries at their
points of weakness, true enough, but often points of
greatest strengths, are, paradoxically, really points of weakness.

~ *Constance M. Wishaw*

One of the hardest things in this world is to admit
you are wrong. And nothing is more helpful in resolving
a situation than its frank admission.

~ *Benjamin Disraeli*

If you board the wrong train, it is no use running
along the corridor in the other direction.

~ *Dietrich Bonhoeffer*

The lame man who keeps the right road
outstrips the runner who takes a wrong one.

~ *Francis Bacon*

A man should never be ashamed to own he has
been in the wrong, which is but saying,
in other words, that he is wiser today than he was yesterday.

~ *Alexander Pope*

The rate at which a person can mature is directly
proportional to the embarrassment he can tolerate.
~ *Douglas Engelbart*

Don't argue for other people's weaknesses. Don't argue for your
own. When you make a mistake, admit it, correct it, and learn
from it — immediately.
~ *Steven Covey*

Almost all our faults are more pardonable than the methods
we resort to to hide them.
~ *François de La Rochefoucauld*

Temper gets you into trouble, pride keeps you there.
~ *Anonymous*

It is a sign of strength, not of weakness,
to admit that you don't know all the answers.
~ *John P. Longhrane*

The only wisdom we can hope to acquire is
the wisdom of humility: humility is endless.
~ *T. S. Eliot*, Four Quartets, "East Coker"

Curiosity is, in great and generous minds, the first passion and the last.
~ *Samuel Johnson*

Curiosity will conquer fear even more than bravery will.
~ *James Stephens*

Above all else: go out with a sense of humor. It is needed armor.
Joy in one's heart and some laughter on one's lips
is a sign that the person down deep has a pretty good grasp of life.
~ *Hugh Sidey*

Common sense and a sense of humor
are the same thing, moving at different speeds.
~ *William James*

There is no defense against adverse fortune
which is so effectual as an habitual sense of humor.
~ *Thomas W. Higginson*

Humor is to life what shock absorbers are to automobiles.
~ *Denis Waitley*

A good laugh and a long sleep are the best cures in the doctor's book.
~ *Irish proverb*

The aim of a joke is not to degrade the human being
but to remind him that he is already degraded.

~ *George Orwell*

Laughter is the shortest distance between two people.

~ *Victor Borge*

A sense of humor judges one's actions and the actions of others
from a wider reference ... and finds them incongruous.
It dampens enthusiasm; it mocks hope; it pardons shortcomings;
it consoles failure. It recommends moderation.

~ *Thornton Wilder*, The Eighth Day

A man isn't poor if he can still laugh.

~ *Raymond Hitchcock*

I do not admire the excess of a virtue like courage unless I see
at the same time an excess of the opposite virtue, as in
Epaminondas, who possessed extreme courage and extreme
kindness.... We show greatness, not by being at one extreme, but
by touching both at once and occupying all the space in between.

~ *Blaise Pascal*

Simplicity and naturalness are the truest marks of distinction.

~ *W. Somerset Maugham*

Simplicity is the ultimate sophistication.

~ *Leonardo da Vinci*

My belief is that in life people will
take you very much at your own reckoning.

~ *Anthony Trollope*

A man came in to thank his boss for a promotion, and,
all in tears, he said: "This is the first good thing that's
happened to me in years." "What?" said his boss,
"You're an unlucky type. Never mind, then. You're fired."

~ *Anonymous*

"Glamour" is assurance. It is a kind of knowing that you
are all right in every way, mentally and physically
and in appearance, and that, whatever the occasion
or the situation, you are equal to it.

~ *Marlene Dietrich*

I have often thought that the best way to define a man's character
would be to seek out the particular mental or moral attitude,
in which, when it came upon him, he felt himself most deeply
and intensely active and alive. At such moments there is a
voice inside which speaks and says: "This is the real me!"

~ *William James*

V.

VALUES

He has achieved success who has lived well,
laughed often and loved much.

~ *Bessie A. Stanley*

To live content with small means; to seek elegance rather than
luxury, and refinement rather than fashion; to be worthy, not
respectable, and wealthy, not rich; to listen to stars and birds,
babes and sages with open heart; to study hard, to think quietly,
act frankly, talk gently, await occasions, hurry never; in a word,
to let the spiritual, unbidden and unconscious, grow up through
the common — this is my symphony.

~ *William Channing*

To laugh often and love much; to win the respect of intelligent
persons and the affection of children; to earn the approbation
of honest citizens and endure the betrayal of false friends;
to appreciate beauty; to find the best in others; to give of one's
self; to leave the world a bit better, whether by a healthy child,
a garden patch or a redeemed social condition; to have played
and laughed with enthusiasm and sung with exultation;
to know even one life has breathed easier because you have lived
— this is to have succeeded.

~ *Ralph Waldo Emerson*

Principles for the Development of a Complete Mind:
Study the science of art. Study the art of science.
Develop your senses — especially learn how to see.
Realize that everything connects to everything else.

~ *Leonardo da Vinci*

That man is the richest whose pleasures are the cheapest.

~ *Henry David Thoreau*

The greatest wealth is a poverty of desires.

~ *Seneca*

The wealth of a man is the number of things which
he loves and blesses, which he is loved and blessed by!

~ *Thomas Carlyle*

So much is a man worth as he esteems himself.

~ *Francois Rabelais*

Nothing can bring you peace, but yourself.

~ *Ralph Waldo Emerson*

We can never have enough of that which we really do not want.

~ *Eric Hoffer*

The real measure of your wealth is
how much you'd be worth if you lost all your money.

~ *Bernard Meltzer*

Do not pursue what is illusory — property and position:
all that is gained at the expense of your nerves decade
after decade and can be confiscated in one fell night.
Live with a steady superiority over life.

~ *Alexander Solzhenitsyn*

Look at every path closely and deliberately. Try it as many
times as you think necessary. This question is one
that only a very old man asks. Does this path have a heart?

~ *Carlos Castaneda*

The price of anything is the amount of life you exchange for it.

~ *Henry David Thoreau*

The happiness of life ... is made up of minute fractions — the
little, soon-forgotten charities of a kiss, a smile, a kind look, a
heartfelt compliment in the disguise of playful raillery, and the
countless infinitesimals of pleasurable thought and genial feeling.

~ *Samuel Taylor Coleridge*

Enjoy the little things, for one day
you may look back and realize they were the big things.

~ *Anonymous*

Hold every moment sacred. Give each clarity and meaning,
each the weight of thine awareness,
each its true and due fulfillment.

~ *Thomas Mann*

Each small task of everyday life is part
of the total harmony of the universe.

~ *St. Theresa of Lisieux*

Look at everything always as though you
were seeing it either for the first or last time.

~ *Betty Smith*

In order to be utterly happy the only thing necessary is to
refrain from comparing this moment with other moments
in the past — which I often did not fully enjoy because
I was comparing them with other moments of the future.

~ *André Gide*

The next message you need is always right where you are.

~ *Ram Dass*

God speaks to every individual through
what happens to him moment by moment.
~ *Jean Pierre de Caussade*

What you are looking for is who is looking.
~ *Saint Francis of Assisi*

One instant is eternity;
eternity is the now.
When you see through this one instant,
you see through the one who sees.
~ *Wu-Men*

The moment one gives close attention to anything,
even a blade of grass, it becomes a mysterious, awesome,
indescribably magnificent world in itself.
~ *Henry Miller*, Grass

You are a phenomenon no less magical than any possibility.
You could just as easily have been born a thousand years
ago in what is now Thailand, or hatched yesterday as a dragonfly.
Why not live as extravagantly as the odds are preposterous
you showed up like this?
~ *D.W. Brown*

Do not wish to be anything but what you are,
and try to be that perfectly.

~ *St. Francis de Sales*

If there is a sin against life, it consists perhaps not so
much in despairing of life as in hoping for another life
and in eluding the implacable grandeur of this life.

~ *Albert Camus*

You are the material itself of the Great Work.

~ *Grillot de Givry*

The only important thing is to follow nature.
A tiger should be a good tiger; a tree, a good tree.
So man should be man. But to know what man is,
one must follow Nature and go on alone,
admitting the importance of the unexpected.
Still, nothing is possible without love.... For love
puts one in a mood to risk everything,
and not to withhold important elements.

~ *Carl Jung*

Give thanks for what you are now,
and keep fighting for what you want to be tomorrow.

~ *Fernanda Miramontes-Landeros*

Not the fruit of experience, but experience itself, is the end.
A counted number of pulses only is given to us of a variegated,
dramatic life…. How shall we pass most swiftly from point
to point, and be present always at the focus where the greatest
number of vital forces unite in their purest energy?

~ *Walter Pater*

To-morrow's life is too late: live to-day.

~ *Martial*

The fool … is always getting ready to live.

~ *Epicurus*

Here's Death, twitching my ear:
"Live," says he, "for I am coming."

~ *Virgil*

Before ever it has uttered or understood,
this admirable and fearful secret of universal existence
will be obliterated and lost

~ *Giacomo Leopardi*

There is no cure for birth or death save to enjoy the interval.

~ *George Santayana*

It began in mystery, and it will end in mystery,
but what a savage and beautiful country lies in between.

~ *Diane Ackerman*

All existence is a perpetual flux of "being and becoming"!

~ *Ernst Haeckel*

For mortals, mortal things. All things leave us.
Or if they do not, then we leave them.

~ *Lucian*

Everything changes; nothing perishes.

~ *Ovid*, Metamorphoses

If you wait for tomorrow, tomorrow comes.
If you don't wait for tomorrow, tomorrow comes.

~ *Senegalese proverb*

Do you know that disease and death must needs overtake us,
no matter what we are doing?
What do you wish to be doing when it overtakes you?

~ *Epictetus*

The thought of suicide is a great consolation.

~ *Friedrich Nietzsche*

This is the one reason why we cannot complain of life;
it keeps no one against his will.

~ *Lucius Seneca*

He who wants to have right without wrong, order without
disorder, does not understand the principles of heaven and earth.
He does not know how things hang together.

~ *Chuang Tzu*

Our life is composed, like the harmony of the world, of contrary
things, also of different tones, sweet and harsh, sharp and flat, soft
and loud. If a musician liked only one kind, what would he have
to say? He must know how to use them together and blend them.
And so must we do with good and evil, which are consubstantial
with our life. Our existence is impossible without this mixture,
and one element is no less necessary for it than the other.

~ *Michel de Montaigne*

The call of death is the call of love. Death can be sweet
if we answer it in the affirmative, if we accept it as one of
the great eternal forms of life and transformation.

~ *Hermann Hesse*

Today is a good day to die,
for all the things of my life are present.

~ *Crazy Horse*

If you don't know how to die, don't worry;
Nature will tell you what to do on the spot,
fully and adequately. She will do this job perfectly
for you; don't bother your head about it.

~ *Michel de Montaigne*

First of all there will appear to you, swifter than lightning,
the luminous splendor of the colorless light of Emptiness,
and that will surround you on all sides. Terrified,
you will want to flee from the radiance, and you may
well lose consciousness. Try to submerge yourself in that light,
giving up all belief in a separate self, all attachment to
your illusory ego. Recognize that the boundless Light of this true
Reality is your own true self.

~ *The Tibetan Book of the Dead*

Everything felt is because of contrast.
If there was no death you couldn't feel alive.

~ *Alan Watts*

If a song didn't end it would just be noise.

~ *Anonymous*

Death is nothing to us, since when we exist there is no death,
and when there is death we do not exist.

~ *Epicurus*

Why should I do anything for posterity?
What's posterity ever done for me?

~ *Groucho Marx*

I intend to live forever. So far, so good.

~ *Steven Wright*

Death is not an event in life: we do not live to experience death.
If we take eternity to mean not infinite temporal
duration but timelessness, then eternal life belongs to those
who live in the present.

~ *Ludwig Wittgenstein*

They who would teach me to die
would at the same time teach me to live.

~ *Euripides*

To mourn for the time when one will be no more is just as absurd
as it would be to mourn over the time when as yet one was not.

~ *Arthur Schopenhauer*

You don't have a soul. You are a Soul. You have a body.

~ *Anonymous*

Annihilation has no terrors for me, because I have already tried it
before I was born — a hundred million years — and I have suffered
more in an hour, in this life, than I remember to have suffered
in the whole hundred million years put together. There was a peace,
a serenity, an absence of all sense of responsibility,
an absence of worry, an absence of care, grief, perplexity;
and the presence of a deep content and unbroken satisfaction in
that hundred million years of holiday which I look back upon
with a tender longing.

~ *Mark Twain*

Death does away with time.

~ *Simone de Beauvoir*

Only a cheap curiosity could desire personal immortality.

~ *Hugo Munsterberg*

This life of yours: it's as if someone let you stay in their mansion
while they were going on a trip. It doesn't matter how long
you thought they'd be gone, you have to take care of the place
and cheerfully give up the keys when they get back.

~ *D.W. Brown*

To die is a debt we must all pay.

~ *Euripides*, Alcestis

Death will find you.
But seek the road which makes death a fulfillment.

~ *Dag Hammarskjold*

❧

They are not long, the weeping and the laughter,
Love and desire and hate:
I think they have no portion in us after
We pass the gate.

They are not long, the days of wine and roses:
Out of a misty dream
Our path emerges for a while, then closes
Within a dream.

~ *Ernest Dowson*, They Are Not Long

From too much love of living,
From hope and fear set free,
We thank with brief thanksgiving
Whatever gods may be
That no man lives forever,
That dead men rise up never;
That even the weariest river
Winds somewhere safe to sea.

~ *Algernon Charles Swinburne*, The Garden of Proserpine

❧

Some children were making sand castles on the beach.
One child kicked another child's castle, destroying part of it,
and the owner of this castle flew into a rage:
"He ruined my castle!" he said. The other children took his side
and they attacked the one who had kicked the castle, hitting him
and throwing sticks and rocks at him. After this, they returned
to their separate castles, now anxious and protective, saying:
"Don't anybody touch this. It's mine." But then the sun set and it
started to get dark. Stars could be seen in the sky and the tide
started coming in, washing up against the castles.
One child stamped on their castle, another pushed theirs over
with both hands. Finally, all the children left the beach and went home.

~ *Anonymous*

VI.
THE FLOW

What we call "I" is just a swinging door
which moves when we inhale and when we exhale.

~ *Shunryu Suzuki*

The butterfly doesn't take it is as a personal achievement,
he just disappears through the trees. You too, kind and humble
and not-even-here, it wasn't in a greedy mood that you saw
the light that belongs to everybody.

~ *Jack Kerouac*, The Scripture of the Golden Eternity

Angels can fly because they can take themselves lightly.

~ *G. K. Chesterton*

Do you see that kitten chasing so prettily her own tail?
If you could look with her eyes you might see her surrounded
by hundreds of figures performing complex dramas, with
tragic and comic issues, long conversations, many characters, many
ups and downs of fate, — and meantime it is only
puss and her tail. How long before our masquerade will end its
noise of tambourines, laughter, and shouting, and we shall
find it was a solitary performance?... What imports it whether
it is Kepler and the sphere, Columbus and America, a reader
and his book, or puss with her tail?

~ *Ralph Waldo Emerson*

Thought is constantly creating problems ... and then trying to
solve them. But as it tries to solve them it makes it worse
because it doesn't notice that it's creating them, and the more it
thinks, the more problems it creates.

~ *David Bohm*

If you want to see the Truth, do not be for or against things.
The struggle between "for" and "against" is the mind's worst disease.
Don't search for Truth, just stop worshipping opinions.
Let things be their own way. Be serene in the oneness of things,
and when doubt arises just say: "Not two."

~ *Seng-ts'an*

A mouse caught hold of a camel's lead rope
in his two forelegs and walked off with it....
The camel went along,
letting the mouse feel heroic.
"Enjoy yourself," he thought.
"There's something I have to teach you."

They came to the edge of a great river.
The mouse was dumbfounded.
"What are you waiting for?
Step forward into the river. You are my leader.
Don't stop here."
"I'm afraid of being drowned."
The camel walked into the water.
"It's only just above the knee."
"*Your* knee! Your knee
is a hundred times over my head!"
"Maybe you shouldn't be leading,"
the Camel replied.

~ *Rumi*

All boundaries are held in common. When you understand this,
you see that the sense of being "me" is exactly
the same sensation as being one with the whole cosmos.
You do not need to go through some other weird, different,
or odd kind of experience to feel in total connection with everything.

~ *Alan Watts*

You do not have to walk on your knees
For a hundred miles through the desert, repenting.
You only have to let the soft animal of your body
love what it loves.

~ Mary Oliver

Two prisoners whose cells adjoin communicate with each other by
knocking on the wall. The wall is the thing which separates them
but is also their means of communication. It is the same with us
and God. Every separation is a link.

~ Simone Weil

Everything in nature is lyrical in its ideal essence, tragic in its fate,
and comic in its existence. Being, then, is the dazzle each of us
makes as we thread the dance of those three rhythms.

~ George Santayana

A student asked his teacher: "Are the mountains and the sky
and everything I see the body of God?"
"Yes," replied the teacher, "but what a pity to say so."

~ Zen story

The attainment of enlightenment from ego's point of view is
extreme death, the death of self, the death of me and mine, the
death of the watcher. It is the ultimate and final disappointment.

~ Chogyam Trungpa

A person who says, "I'm enlightened," probably isn't.

~ *Ram Dass*

What could be more dualistic than saying dualism is wrong?

~ *Richard Smoley*

Asking "What am I doing with my life?"
is like trying to put a horse on top of a horse and then ride it.

~ *Suzuki Roshi*

The Great Way has no gate. Clear water has no taste.
The tongue has no bone.
In complete stillness, a stone girl is dancing.

~ *Seung Sahn*

Two men were arguing about a flag flapping in the wind.
"It's the wind that is really moving," stated the first one.
"No, it is the flag that is moving," contended the second.
Someone who happened to be walking by, overheard the debate
and interrupted them. "Neither the flag nor the wind is moving,"
he said, "It is *mind* that moves."

~ *Zen story*

When you try to stop activity to achieve passivity
your very effort fills you with activity.

~ *Xinxin Ming*

[Meditation] is exactly like muddy water
left to stand in a glass. Little by little, the sediment sinks
to the bottom and the water becomes pure.

~ *Taisen Deshimaru*

The mind of a perfect man is like a mirror. It grasps nothing.
It expects nothing. It reflects, but it does not hold.

~ *Chung Tzu*

The hearing that is only in the ears is one thing. The hearing of
the understanding is another. But the hearing of the spirit is
not limited to any one faculty, to the ear, or to the mind. Hence,
it demands the emptiness of all the faculties. And when the
faculties are empty, then the whole being listens. There is then
a direct grasp of what is right there before you that can never
be heard with the ear or understood with the mind.

~ *Chung Tzu*

When you look for it, there is nothing to see. When you listen for
it, there is nothing to hear. When you use it, it is inexhaustible.

~ *Lao Tzu*

What you see is not the plant,
but a history of what the plant has been doing.

~ *Anonymous*

With expectation you experience limitation;
without expectation you experience subtlety.

~ *Lao Tzu*

If only I could leave everything as it is,
without moving a single star or a single cloud. Oh, if only I could!

~ *Antonio Porchia*

No snowflake ever falls in the wrong place.

~ *Anonymous*

You can't have everything. Where would you put it?

~ *Steven Wright*

The river pulls you (yin) and pushes you (yang), but it is one river.

~ *Walter George*

When a contradiction is impossible to resolve except by a lie,
then we know that it is really a door.

~ *Simone Weil*

We shall not cease from exploration
And the end of all our exploring
Will be to arrive where we started
And know it for the first time.

~ *T. S. Eliot*, Little Gidding

I know what the great cure is: it is to give up, to relinquish,
to surrender, so that our little hearts may beat in unison
with the great heart of the world.

~ *Henry Miller*

Would you prefer the happiness of scratching a mosquito
bite over the happiness of not having a mosquito bite in
the first place?

~ *Sogyal Rinpoche*

A traveling salesman saw a farmer holding a little pig up
to a plum tree to feed him plums, and he stopped and asked,
"Wouldn't it save time to just pick the plums and then give
them to the pig?" The farmer shrugged and replied:
"What's time to a pig?"

~ *old joke*

Silence is God's first language.
Everything else is a poor translation.

~ *Thomas Keating*

As my prayers became more attentive and inward,
I had less and less to say. I finally became completely silent....
This is how it is. To pray does not mean to listen
to oneself speaking. Prayer involves becoming silent,
and being silent, and waiting until God is heard.

~ *Søren Kierkegaard*

The hen does not lay eggs in the marketplace.

~ *Sufi proverb*

The soul contemplates herself in the mirror of Divinity.
God Himself is the mirror, which he conceals from whom He will,
and uncovers to whom He will.... The more the soul is able
to transcend all words, the more it approaches the mirror.

~ *Meister Eckhart*

Quiet makes quiet.

~ *Anonymous*

I saw heaven. In it nothing ever happened, the events of a
million years ago were just as phantom and ungraspable
as the events of now, or the events of the next ten minutes.
It was perfect ... something surely humble.

~ *Jack Kerouac*

The wild geese do not intend to cast their reflection,
The water has no mind to receive their image.

~ *Zen reflection*

An old pond,
The sound of the water
When a frog jumps in.

~ *Matsuo Bashô*

VII.
{ LOVE }

Seldom need the heart be lonely,
If it finds a lonelier still;
Self-forgetting, seeking only
Emptier cups of love to fill.

~ *Frances Ridley Havergal*

What wisdom can you find that is greater than kindness?

~ *Jean-Jacques Rousseau*

Forgive what seems to be the harm done to yourself;
Put up with difficult people;
Pray for whatever has life.

~ *James K. Baxter*

[The human spirit] has come to believe that compassion,
in which all ethics must take root, can only attain its
full breadth and depth if it embraces all living creatures
and does not limit itself to mankind.

~ *Albert Schweitzer*

I care not much for a man's religion
whose dog or cat are not the better for it.

~ *Abraham Lincoln*

One act of beneficence, one act of real usefulness,
is worth all the abstract sentiment in the world.

~ *Anne Radcliff*

You can't live a perfect day until you do something
for someone who will never be able to repay you.

~ *John Wooden*

Beginning today, treat everyone you meet
as if they were going to be dead by midnight.

~ *Og Mandino*

A boy doesn't have to go to war to be a hero; he can say he
doesn't like pie when he sees there isn't enough to go around.

~ *Edgar Watson Howe*

To complain that life has no joys while there is a single creature
whom we can relieve by our bounty, assist by our counsels
or enliven by our presence, is to lament the loss of that which
we possess, and is just as irrational as to die of thirst with the
cup in our hands.

~ *Thomas Fitzosborne*

If you don't find God in the next person you meet,
it is a waste of time looking for him further.

~ *Mahatma Gandhi*

If you help others, you will be helped, perhaps tomorrow, perhaps
in one hundred years, but you will be helped. Nature must pay off
the debt. It is a mathematical law and all life is mathematics.

~ *G. I. Gurdjieff*

We are here on Earth to do good to others.
What the others are here for, I don't know.

~ *W. H. Auden*

The service we render to others is really the rent we pay
for our room on this earth.

~ *Wilfred Grenfell*

Keep your fears to yourself but share your courage with others.
~ *Robert Louis Stevenson*

Pretend that every single person you meet has a sign
around his or her neck that says, "Make me feel important."
~ *Mary Kay Ash*

Thousands of candles can be lit from a single candle,
and the life of the candle will not be shortened.
Happiness never decreases by being shared.
~ *Buddha*

We are cups, constantly and quietly being filled.
The trick is, knowing how to tip
ourselves over and let the beautiful stuff out.
~ *Ray Bradbury*

Even in the time of elephantine vanity and greed,
one never has to look far to see the campfires of gentle people.
Lacking any other purpose in life,
it would be good enough to live for their sake.
~ *Garrison Keillor*

If heaven made him, earth can find some use for him.
~ *Anonymous*

It is no surprise
that danger and suffering surround us.
What astonishes is the singing.

~ *Jack Gilbert*

Do not inflict your will.
Just give love.
The soul will take that love
and put it where it can best be used.

~ *Emmanuel*

What I cannot love, I overlook.

~ *Anaïs Nin*

What is tolerance? It is the consequence of humanity.
We are all formed of frailty and error; let us pardon reciprocally
each other's folly — that is the first law of nature.

~ *Voltaire*

With no matter what human being, taken individually, I always
find reasons for concluding that sorrow and misfortune do not
suit him; either because he seems too mediocre for anything so
great, or, on the contrary, too precious to be destroyed.

~ *Simone Weil*

To be angry at people means that one considers their acts
to be important. It is imperative to cease to feel that way.
The acts of men cannot be important enough to offset our
only viable alternative: our unchangeable encounter with infinity.

~ *Carlos Castaneda*

Do not ask me to be kind; just ask me to act as if I were.

~ *Jules Renard*

Always go to other people's funerals, otherwise they won't go to yours.

~ *Yogi Berra*

We have no more right to put our discordant states of mind into
the lives of those around us and rob them of their sunshine and
brightness than we have to enter their house and steal their silverware.

~ *Julia Seton*

Even in my worst moments I would not destroy a Greek statue
or a fresco by Giotto. Why anything else then? Why, for example,
a moment in the life of a human being who could have been
happy for that moment.

~ *Simone Weil*

I destroy my enemy when I make him my friend.

~ *Abraham Lincoln*

The first duty of love is to listen.

~ *Paul Tillich*

If you can't be kind, be vague.

~ *Anonymous*

When a friend is in trouble, don't annoy him by asking if there is anything you can do. Think up something appropriate and do it.

~ *Edgar Watson Howe*

Good company on the road is the shortest cut.

~ *Ralph Waldo Emerson*

It is not so much our friends' help that helps us, as it is the confidence of their help.

~ *Epicurus*

The hard and stiff will be broken.
The soft and supple will prevail.

~ *Lao Tzu*

Soft is stronger than hard, water stronger than rock, love stronger than violence.

~ *Hermann Hesse*, Siddhartha

Man has bought brains, but all the millions in the world
have failed to buy love. Man has subdued bodies,
but all the power on earth has been unable to subdue love....
High on a throne, with all the splendor and pomp
his gold can command, man is yet poor and desolate,
if love passes him by. And if it stays, the poorest hovel
is radiant with warmth, life and color.

~ *Emma Goldman*

May the nourishment of the earth be yours,
may the clarity of light be yours,
may the fluency of the ocean be yours,
may the protection of the ancestors be yours.
And so may a slow
wind work these words
of love around you,
an invisible cloak
to mind your life.

~ *Gaelic Blessing*

Today I forgive all those who have ever offended me.
I give my love to all thirsty hearts, both to those who love me
and those who do not love me.

~ *Paramahansa Yogananda*

Forgiveness is the final form of love.

~ *Reinhold Niebuhr*

Love your enemy.

~ *Hebrew proverb*

If we could read the secret history of our enemies,
we should find in each man's life sorrow
and suffering enough to disarm all hostility.

~ *Henry Wadsworth Longfellow*

I have decided to stick with love.
Hate is too great a burden to bear.

~ *Martin Luther King*

Holding on to anger is like grasping a hot coal
with the intent of throwing it at someone else.

~ *Buddha*

Before you embark on a journey of revenge —
dig two graves.

~ *Confucius*

I will permit no person to narrow and
degrade my soul by making me hate them.

~ *Booker T. Washington*

There's not enough time to be nasty.

~ *Desmond Tutu*

[Hatred is] a precious liquid,
a poison dearer than that of the Borgias —
because it is made from our blood, our health,
our sleep, and two-thirds of our love —
we must be stingy with it.

~ *Charles Baudelaire*

To forgive is to set a prisoner free and discover that the prisoner was you.

~ *Lewis B. Smedes*

Forgiveness means giving up all hope for a better past.

~ *Lily Tomlin*

The only way you may correct the bad things in
your past is to add better things to your future.

~ *Shiloh Morrison*

The most tragic thing in the world and in life ... is love.
Love is the child of illusion and the parent of disillusion;
love is consolation in desolation; it is the sole medicine
against death, for it's death's brother.

~ *Miguel De Unamuno*

There is a land of the living and a land of the dead
and the bridge is love, the only survival, the only meaning.

~ *Thornton Wilder*, The Bridge of San Luis Rey

The eye through which I see God is the same eye through
which God sees me; my eye and God's eye are one eye,
one seeing, one knowing, one love.

~ *Meister Eckhart*

If you want to be found, stand where the seeker seeks.

~ *Sidney Lanier*

Be blinding or invisible, nothing in between.

~ *Anonymous*

Every child comes with the message that God
is not yet discouraged of man.

~ *Rabindranath Tagore*

Open your eyes! The world is still intact;
it is as pristine as it was on the first day, as fresh as milk!

~ *Paul Claudel*

Try to keep your soul young and quivering right up to old age,
and to imagine right up to the brink of death that life is only
beginning.... I think that is the only way to keep adding to one's
talent, to one's affections, and one's inner happiness.

~ *George Sand*

For there was that law of life so cruel and
so just which demanded that one must grow
or else pay more for remaining the same.

~ *Norman Mailer*

Inside every older person is a younger person —
wondering what the hell happened.

~ *Cora Harvey Armstrong*

You can judge your age by the amount of pain you feel
when you come in contact with a new idea.

~ *Pearl S. Buck*

The second half of a man's life is made up of nothing
but the habits he has acquired during the first half.

~ *Fyodor Dostoevsky*

Oh, would that my mind could let fall its dead ideas,
as the tree does its withered leaves!

~ *Andre Gide*

There is in a person an upwelling spring of life, energy,
love, whatever you like to call it. If a course is not cut for it,
it turns the ground round it into a swamp.

~ *Mark Rutherford*

What cannot go forward — slips back.

~ *Gaius V. Paterculus*

We cannot solve our problems with the
same thinking we used when we created them.

~ *Albert Einstein*

Ignorance is the womb of monsters.

~ *Henry Ward Beecher*

When Thought is clos'd in Caves.
Then love shall shew its root in deepest hell.

~ *William Blake*, Jerusalem

As far as we can discern, the sole purpose of human existence
is to kindle a light in the darkness of mere being.

~ *Carl Jung*

ॐ

Be careful how you interpret the world: it is like that.

~ *Erich Heller*

The world is like a mirror; frown at it,
and it frowns at you. Smile and it smiles, too.

~ *Herbert Samuels*

The words "I am…" are potent words; be careful
what you hitch them to. The thing you're claiming has
a way of reaching back and claiming you.

~ *A. L. Kitselman*

A person will worship something
— have no doubt about that.

We may think our tribute is paid in
secret in the dark recesses of our
hearts, but it will out.

That which dominates our
imaginations and our thoughts will
determine our lives, and character.

Therefore, it behooves us to be
careful what we worship, for what we
are worshipping we are becoming.

~ *Ralph Waldo Emerson*

Whatever the self describes, describes the self.

~ *Jacob Boehme*

We don't see things as they are, we see them as we are.

~ *Qur'an*

People seem not to see that their opinion of the world
is also a confession of character.

~ *Ralph Waldo Emerson*

Once upon a time a man whose ax was missing suspected his
neighbor's son. The boy walked like a thief, looked like a thief,
and spoke like a thief. But the man found his ax while digging in
the valley, and the next time he saw his neighbor's son, the boy
walked, looked and spoke like any other child.

~ *Lao Tzu*

When you hate someone, the way they hold their spoon
annoys you; when you love someone, they can spill a bowl
of soup in your lap and you don't mind.

~ *Anonymous*

A thankful person is thankful under all circumstances.
A complaining soul complains even if he lives in paradise.

~ *Baha'u'llah*

You will become as small as your controlling desire;
as great as your dominant aspiration.

~ *James Lane Allen*

If the only prayer you said in your whole life was,
"thank you," that would suffice.

~ *Meister Eckhart*

Sincerity is the fulfillment
of our own nature,
and to arrive at it we need
only follow our own true Self.
Sincerity is the beginning
and end of existence;
without it, nothing can endure.
Therefore the mature person
values sincerity above all things.

~ *Tzu-Ssu*

A horse being whipped to keep going up a mountain so that
it can carry a child to life-saving medical attention does not
understand the purpose of its suffering. Isn't it possible that our
suffering might also serve a purpose that we cannot grasp?

~ *Viktor Frankl*

All nature is but art, unknown to thee;
All chance, direction, which thou canst not see;
All discord, harmony, not understood;
All partial evil, universal good:
And, spite of pride, in erring reason's spite,
One truth is clear, whatever IS, is RIGHT.

~ *Alexander Pope*, Essay on Man

The cut worm forgives the plow.

~ *William Blake*, The Marriage of Heaven and Hell

Let your soul stand cool and composed before a million universes.
~ *Walt Whitman*

The will of God will not take you where
the grace of God cannot keep you.
~ *Anonymous*

There is no coming to consciousness without pain.
~ *Carl Jung*

Who ne'er his bread in sorrow, ate,
Who ne'er the mournful midnight hours
Weeping upon his bed has sate,
He knows not you, ye Heavenly Powers.
~ *Johann Wolfgang von Goethe*

Everything great in the world comes from neurotics. They
alone have founded our religions and composed our masterpieces.
Never will the world know all it owes them nor all they have
suffered to enrich us. We enjoy lovely music, beautiful paintings,
a thousand intellectual delicacies, but we have no idea of their
cost, to those who invented them, in sleepless nights, tears,
spasmodic laughter, rashes, asthmas, epilepsies, and the fear of
death, which is worse than all the rest.
~ *Marcel Proust*

What is this darkness? What is its name?
Call it: an aptitude for sensitivity. Call it:
a rich sensitivity which will make you whole.
Call it: your potential for vulnerability.
~ *Meister Eckhart*

The beauty of the world ... has two edges, one of laughter,
one of anguish, cutting the heart asunder.
~ *Virginia Woolf*, A Room of One's Own

There is a palace that opens only to tears.
~ *Zohar*

We must embrace pain and burn it as fuel for our journey.
~ *Kenji Miyazawa*

Acceptance of what has happened is the first step
to overcoming the consequences of any misfortune.
~ *William James*

And even in our sleep, pain that cannot forget falls
drop by drop upon the heart, and in our own despite,
against our will, comes wisdom to us by the awful grace of God.
~ *Aeschylus*, Agamemnon

When an apprentice gets hurt, or complains of being tired,
the workmen … have this fine expression:
"It is the trade entering his body."
Each time that we have some pain to go through,
we can say to ourselves quite truly that it is the universe,
the order and beauty of the world, and obedience of
creation to God that are entering our body.

~ *Simone Weil*

The world breaks everyone and afterward
many are strong at the broken places.

~ *Ernest Hemingway*, A Farewell To Arms

When you are sorrowful look again in your heart,
and you shall see that in truth you are weeping for that
which has been your delight.

~ *Kahlil Gibran*

What we once enjoyed and deeply loved we can never lose.
For all that we love deeply becomes a part of us.

~ *Helen Keller*

Never anticipate evils; or, because you cannot have
things exactly as you wish, make them out worse than
they are through spite and willfulness.

~ *William Hazlitt*

He who fears he will suffer, already suffers from his fear.

~ *Michel de Montaigne*

The chief pang of most trials is not so much the
actual suffering itself as our own spirit of resistance to it.

~ *Jean Nicolas Grou*

Let life happen to you. Believe me: life is in the right, always.

~ *Rainer Maria Rilke*

A bitter pill is better swallowed than chewed.

~ *C. M. Mayo*

He who has a why to live, can bear with almost any how.

~ *Viktor Frankl*

What was hard to endure is sweet to recall.

~ *English proverb*

The best bridge between hope and
despair is often a good night's sleep.

~ *Anonymous*

This, too, shall pass.

~ *Anonymous*

Life is hard? Next to what?

~ *Anonymous*

Don't ask for fair. You don't want fair.

~ *John MacArthur*

The world owes you nothing. It was here first.

~ *Mark Twain*

[Despair is] the absolute extreme of self-love.
It is reached when a man deliberately turns his back
on all help from anyone else in order to taste the
rotten luxury of knowing himself to be lost.

~ *Thomas Merton*

The unhappy person resents it when you try to
cheer him up, because that means he has to stop
dwelling on himself and start paying attention
to the universe.

~ *Tom Robbins*, Jitterbug Perfume

The attitude of unhappiness is not only painful,
it is mean and ugly.... It but fastens and perpetuates
the trouble which occasioned it, and increases the
total evil of the situation. At all costs, then, we
ought to reduce the sway of that mood; we ought to
scout it in ourselves and others, and never show it tolerance.

~ *William James*

A person who hates himself loves himself as a self-hater.

~ *Susan Sontag*

Keep a green tree in your heart and perhaps the singing bird will come.

~ *Chinese proverb*

It doesn't hurt to be optimistic. You can always cry later.

~ *Lucimar Santos de Lima*

In the long run, the pessimist may be proved right;
but the optimist has a better time on the trip.

~ *Daniel L. Reardon*

A cynic is not merely one who reads bitter lessons from the past,
he is one who is prematurely disappointed in the future.

~ *Sidney J. Harris*

If God adds another day to our life, let us receive it gladly.

~ *Marcus Annaeus Seneca*

I make the most of all that comes and the least of all that goes.

~ *Sara Teasdale*

Don't curse the darkness, light a candle.

~ *Chinese proverb*

There is not enough darkness in all the world
to put out the light of even one small candle.

~ *Robert Alden*

Those who understand see themselves in all,
and all, in themselves.

~ *Bhagavad Gita*

Life delights in life.

~ *William Blake*

Every blade of grass has its angel that bends
over it and whispers, "Grow, grow."

~ *Talmud*

For the thing-in-itself, the will to live, exists whole and
undivided in every being, even in the smallest, as completely
as in the sum-total of all things that ever were or are or will be.

~ *Arthur Schopenhauer*

Even stones have a love, a love that seeks the ground.

~ *Meister Eckhart*

You do not need to leave your room. Remain sitting at
your table and listen. Do not even listen, simply wait.
Do not even wait, be quite still and solitary.
The world will freely offer itself to you to be unmasked,
it has no choice; it will roll in ecstasy at your feet.

~ *Franz Kafka*

God must act and pour Himself into you the moment
He finds you ready … just as when the air is clear
and pure the sun has to burst forth and cannot refrain.

~ *Meister Eckhart*

To recognize our own divinity, and our intimate relation to
the Universal, is to attach the belts of our machinery to the powerhouse
of the Universe. One need remain in hell no longer than one
chooses to; we can rise to any heaven we ourselves choose; and when we
choose so to rise, all the higher powers of the Universe combine to
help us heavenward.

~ *Henry James*

The most exquisite paradox ... as soon as you give it all up, you can have it all. As long as you want power, you can't have it. The minute you don't want power, you'll have more than you ever dreamed possible.

~ *Ram Dass*

By means of all created things, without exception,
the divine assails us, penetrates us and moulds us.
We imagined it as distant and inaccessible, whereas in fact
we live steeped in its burning layers.

~ *Pierre Teilhard de Chardin*

Teach us to care and not to care
Teach us to sit still
Even among these rocks,
Our peace in His will.

~ *T. S. Eliot*, Ash Wednesday

God does not give us everything we want,
but He does fulfill his promises,
leading us along the best and
straightest paths to himself.

~ *Dietrich Bonhoeffer*

Lord, make me an instrument of your peace.
Where there is hatred, let me sow love.
Where there is injury, pardon.
Where there is doubt, faith.
Where there is despair, hope.
Where there is darkness, light.
Where there is sadness, joy.
O Divine Master,
grant that I may not so much seek to be consoled, as to console;
to be understood, as to understand;
to be loved, as to love.
For it is in giving that we receive.
It is in pardoning that we are pardoned,
and it is in dying that we are born to Eternal Life.

~ *Saint Francis*

Hear our prayer, O God, for our friends the animals,
especially for animals who are suffering; for any that are hunted
or lost or deserted or frightened or hungry; for all that
must be put to sleep. We entreat for them all Thy mercy and pity,
and for those who deal with them we ask a heart of compassion
and gentle hands and kindly words. Make us true friends to
animals and so to share the blessings of the merciful.

~ *Albert Schweitzer*

Give us Lord, a bit o' sun,
A bit o' work and a bit o' fun;
Give us all in the struggle and sputter,
Our daily bread and a bit o' butter.

~ *Anonymous*

The good man's past begins to change so that his forgiven
sins and remembered sorrows take on the quality of heaven.
At the end of all things, the blessed will say, "We never lived
anywhere but in heaven."

~ *C. S. Lewis*, The Great Divorce

And the stars down so close, and sadness and pleasure so
close together, really the same thing ... the stars are close
and dear and I have joined the brotherhood of the worlds.
And everything's holy — everything, even me.

~ *John Steinbeck*, The Grapes of Wrath

Even a thought, even a possibility can shatter and transform us.

~ *Marcus Aurelius*

Every action of our lives touches on some chord
that will vibrate in eternity.

~ *Edwin Hubbel Chapin*

There is only the moment, and yet the moment is always
giving way to the next, so that there is not even Now,
there is Nothing. True, true. There is nothing, if that is
the way to understand how much there is.

~ *M. C. Richards*

If it were not God's will, it wouldn't exist even for an instant;
so if something happens, it must be his will.
If you truly enjoyed God's will, you would feel exactly as
though you were in the kingdom of heaven, whatever
happened to you or didn't happen to you.

~ *Meister Eckhart*

There is no effort in what is divine.

~ *Aeschylus*

To renounce our position as the center of the world,
not only intellectually, but in our imagination, as well,
is to awaken to what is real and eternal. It is to see the
true light and hear the true silence. To abandon our false
divinity and see that all points are equally centers, that the
true center is outside this world, this is our free choice.
Such consent is love, and the image of this love is the love
of our neighbor and the love of beauty.

~ *Simone Weil*

Let go of this everywhere and this something, in exchange
for this nowhere and nothing. This nothing may be
better felt than seen because we are blinded by the magnitude
of its spiritual light. Drive into that dense cloud of
unknowing with a sharp spear of longing love.

~ *Anonymous*, The Cloud of Unknowing

Let's pretend there's a way of getting through into it, somehow.
Let's pretend the glass has got all soft like gauze, so that we
can get through. Why, it's turning into a sort of mist now,
I declare! It'll be easy enough to get through.

~ *Lewis Carroll*, Through the Looking Glass

We need to find God, and he cannot be found in noise and
restlessness. God is the friend of silence. See how nature — trees,
flowers, grass — grows in silence; see the stars, the moon and the
sun, how they move in silence....

~ *Mother Teresa*

There is something formless and perfect that was here
before the universe was born. It is serene, unchanging, infinite.
It was never born, so it can never die.
It has no desires for itself, so it is present for all beings.

~ *Lao Tzu*

Whilst everything around me is ever-changing, ever-dying,
there is underlying all that change a living power
that is changeless, that holds together, that creates, dissolves,
and recreates. That informing power or spirit is God.
And since nothing else I see merely through the senses can
or will persist, He alone is.

~ *Mahatma Gandhi*

You never enjoy the world aright, till the Sea itself
floweth in your veins, till you are clothed with the
heavens and crowned with the stars ... till you love men
so as to desire their happiness with a thirst equal to
the zeal of your own; till you delight in God for being
good to all: you never enjoy the world.

~ *Thomas Traherne*

God wants nothing of you but the gift of a peaceful heart.

~ *Meister Eckhart*

And what is the end of the whole matter?
As if honey could taste itself and all its drops together
and all its drops could taste each other and each the
whole honeycomb as itself, so should the end be
with God and the soul of man and the universe.

~ *Sri Aurobindo*

That is perfect. This is perfect. Perfect comes from perfect.
Take perfect from perfect, the remainder is perfect.
May peace and peace and peace be everywhere.

~ *Upanishads*

I entered and beheld with the eye of my soul.
the Light Unchangeable.

~ *St. Augustine*

All calm, as it was bright.

~ *Henry Vaughn*

Let nothing stand between you and the light.

~ *Henry David Thoreau*

VIII.

"Desiderata"
Max Ehrmann (1872–1945)

Go placidly amid the noise and haste,
and remember what peace there may be in silence.
As far as possible, without surrender, be on good terms
with all persons. Speak your truth quietly and clearly;
and listen to others, even to the dull and ignorant;
they too have their story.

Avoid loud and aggressive persons; they are vexatious to the spirit.
If you compare yourself with others, you may become vain or bitter,
for always there will be greater and lesser persons than yourself.
Enjoy your achievements as well as your plans.
Keep interested in your own career, however humble;
it is a real possession in the changing fortunes of time.
Exercise caution in your business affairs, for the
world is full of trickery. But let this not blind you to what
virtue there is; many persons strive for high ideals,
and everywhere life is full of heroism. Be yourself.

Especially, do not feign affection. Neither be cynical about love;
for in the face of all aridity and disenchantment,
it is as perennial as the grass. Take kindly the counsel of the years,
gracefully surrendering the things of youth.

Nurture strength of spirit to shield you in sudden misfortune.
But do not distress yourself with dark imaginings.
Many fears are born of fatigue and loneliness.
Beyond a wholesome discipline, be gentle with yourself.
You are a child of the universe no less than the trees and the stars;
you have a right to be here. And whether or not it is clear to you,
no doubt the universe is unfolding as it should.

Therefore be at peace with God, whatever you conceive Him to
be. And whatever your labors and aspirations, in the
noisy confusion of life, keep peace with your soul.
With all its sham, drudgery and broken dreams, it is still a
beautiful world. Be cheerful. Strive to be Happy.

"A Psalm Of Life"
Henry Wadsworth Longfellow (1807–1882)

Tell me not, in mournful numbers,
Life is but an empty dream!
For the soul is dead that slumbers,
And things are not what they seem.

Life is real! Life is earnest!
And the grave is not its goal;
Dust thou art, to dust returnest,
Was not spoken of the soul.

Not enjoyment, and not sorrow,
Is our destined end or way;
But to act, that each to-morrow
Find us farther than to-day.

Art is long, and Time is fleeting,
And our hearts, though stout and brave,
Still, like muffled drums, are beating
Funeral marches to the grave.

In the world's broad field of battle,
In the bivouac of Life,
Be not like dumb, driven cattle!
Be a hero in the strife!

Trust no Future, howe'er pleasant!
Let the dead Past bury its dead!
Act, — act in the living Present!
Heart within, and God o'erhead!

Lives of great men all remind us
We can make our lives sublime,
And, departing, leave behind us
Footprints on the sands of time; —

Footprints, that perhaps another,
Sailing o'er life's solemn main,
A forlorn and shipwrecked brother,
Seeing, shall take heart again.

Let us, then, be up and doing,
With a heart for any fate;
Still achieving, still pursuing,
Learn to labor and to wait.

IX.

from
Johann Wolfgang von Goethe (1749–1832)

Hold onto the present. Every condition,
every moment, is of infinite worth
because it represents Eternity.

Plunge boldly into the thick of life!
Seize it where you will, it is interesting.

Live dangerously, and you live right.

One's inner life is only awakened by the outer,
not by cold calculation,
which only dries up the sap of life.

A person's work is like that of a swimmer.
Ahead lies a body of water that threatens to
swallow you and, if you don't face it bravely,
it will do just that. But through constant,

wise defiance and battle, it loyally supports you,
carries you, and is won.

What matters is doing the right thing.
Whether the right thing happens
or not shouldn't concern you.

The deed is everything, the glory nothing.

There is no situation that cannot be
ennobled by either work or endurance.

Pain and pleasure, good and evil,
often come from unexpected sources.
What does this teach us? To live with
humility and peaceful resignation.

Individuality seems to be Nature's whole aim —
and yet she cares nothing for individuals.

All that is living tends toward color, individuality,
specificity, effectiveness and opacity.
What is dead tends toward knowledge, abstraction,
generality, and transparency.

Life has the talent for fitting in with the most
diverse conditions, but still maintaining its
distinctiveness in doing so.

A man's deepest contentment will come
from attempting to fathom what can be fathomed,
and honoring in silence what cannot be fathomed.

People show their characters most clearly in
what they find laughable. The trouble is small,
the fun is great.

If you take life too glumly, what good is it?
If the morning does not wake you ready for
new delights and the evening leaves you with no
joys to hope for, what's the point of all this
dressing and undressing? Is the sun shining so you can
brood over yesterday or fret over tomorrow's destiny?
Happiness is a ball we run after wherever it rolls,
and when it stops we kick it.

We have in our natures an organ for cynicism
and discontent. The more we feed it, the stronger
it becomes, until it changes from an organ into an
active cancer, corrupting the healthy tissues around it.
Remorse and reproach sets in. We become uncivil to
everyone, including ourselves, we lose the pleasure in
good fortune, others and our own. In desperation we
try to blame the ugliness on something, anything,
outside ourselves, so as not to bear the humility of
our own self-destructiveness.

If we put ourselves in the place of other people,
the jealousy and contempt we feel about them
often disappears, and, if we imagine others in our place,
our pride and conceit can be much diminished.

Always be on the lookout for the merits of your opponents.

Treat people as if they were what they ought to be,
and you contribute to their becoming what they
are capable of becoming.

Every excellent thing makes us uncomfortable at first
because we feel unable to live up to it. Only after habit brings
us to embrace it as belonging to our own sensibilities do
we come to love and value it. It's no wonder we usually prefer to
surround ourselves with mediocrity; it leaves us in peace and gives
us the cozy feeling of keeping company with what is familiar.
The best fortune that can happen to a person
is anything that corrects his or her shortcomings.

I have learned a great deal from illness that I
never could have learned any other way.

There is no past that we can bring back by longing
for it. There is only an eternally new now that builds
and creates itself out of what is best as the past withdraws.

Love has power to give in a moment what toil
can scarcely reach in an age.

X.

ह्ळ

from
Baltasar Gracian (1601–1658)

Be a saint.

All you will ever own is your virtue, everything else is a gift that can be taken away in a moment. Virtue alone is real.

Aspire to a certain gracefulness. Difficult to define, the French call it *je ne sais quoi* — it is a kind of sparkle, gallantry and zest; a wholeheartedness imbued with humor. It is carrying oneself with flair and pluck, a spontaneous ease and a light elegance.

Don't rush headlong into trouble, but go to meet it halfway.

Do the easy as though it were difficult, and the difficult as though it were easy. Be fully present and involved with what is routine; yet, in moments of greatest challenge, when your course is clear, don't think, just act.

Use human means as if there were no divine ones, and divine means as if there were no human ones.

Avoid what is vulgar not because of how others condemn you so much as how your own, better self condemns you.

Go to the good. The bee and the fly both enter the same garden, but one puts his tongue to nectar and the other to dung.

Good taste is knowing how to enjoy something when it is at its most ready.

Learn how to take things. A knife taken by the blade will cut you, but taken by the handle it can be used as a tool.

A good person can be forced to go to war, but not to fight dishonorably. A person of substance does not forget who they are because of what others do; they know who their teachers are.

Be free to speak well of someone who speaks ill of you.

Some things should be laughed off with a gentle humor even if other people are more grave about them. Nothing is sillier than to take everything seriously.

Examine your motives from the other person's perspective. This helps to judge matters more fairly and not to blindly justify yourself.

The person most dangerous to you is yourself.

We are quick to defend ourselves and avoid responsibility by taking a false pleasure in our weaknesses. An affection for your faults is two faults in one.

Anyone can stumble and fall, but a great person won't lie there and make it home.

Flattery is more dangerous than criticism because it covers the faults that criticism will reveal.

A loyal friend should feel free to advise and reprimand if necessary. Someone who always agrees with you isn't showing that they love you, only that they love themselves.

The first thing to do when you are upset is to notice that you are. There is always time to say something, never enough to take it back.

Be firm in your will, not in your judgment.

Most objectives are not achieved because they are not really pursued. People with modest talents who fully apply themselves get further than superior people who don't. A lack of commitment creates more failure than poor execution. Follow through and finish strong. Don't just stalk your prey, make the kill.

Don't save your calculation and foresight until a difficult situation is upon you. Anticipate problems to avoid them. It's easier to hide from danger than to battle it, and you can fend off a blow more easily when you expect one.

Leave the door always open for reconciliation. The pleasure of revenge often becomes pain for the injury we have caused another. Show an openness to receive greater and greater things.

Stay close to the wise and accomplished, good fortune visits them regularly.

Don't let your feelings for the unfortunate
make you one of them.

Hide the wounded finger, it tends to get hit again.
Those with bad intent will exploit a weakness
and the sympathy of our friends rarely helps.
Nobody really wants to hear about it.

Better to be cheated by the price than by
the quality of the merchandise.

Tools often deteriorate more from lack of use than over use.

Hide your caution so that it doesn't hurt your
reputation or arouse suspicion. Just or not,
if you're openly skeptical about the truthfulness of others,
it indicates that you yourself might be deceitful.

If possible, when giving advice, act as if you're reminding
a person of something they forgot.

Keep expectations alive. You are more highly valued
when people have to guess at the extent of your resources,
no matter how great in truth they might be. What's real
can rarely equal what is imagined. The imagination
rushes ahead and makes of things not just what they are,
but what they might be, and what is mysterious is honored.

Don't refuse someone bluntly. Even when you're certain
the answer is "no," it's usually kinder to let their
disappointment come gradually with, "I don't think it's likely."

Know when to leave a situation alone.
A muddied stream can't be made clear by your effort.

Remember to forget. Don't hold to heart what should
be ignored. The best remedy for troubles is often to
forget them. Train you memory and teach it manners.

Shape your imagination.
All happiness in life is dependent on the imagination.

Learn your talents and adjust to reality. Discover what
talent you excel at and apply special effort there.
If you lack strength, use specificity. If nature holds
back her gifts, apply persistence to acquire skills.

Maintain a stout heart. There is no better companion
in a difficult situation than a strong heart.

XI.

from
Marcus Aurelius (21-180)

Work at what's in front of you with the tools you have,
shrinking from nothing, following right reason and
moving towards a more integrated life. Do it vigorously

and with no distractions, yet calmly and with all of your
love and humor. If you seek to keep your divine part
pure, obliged to give it back at any moment, and embrace
what you get, working justly, soberly, and considerately,
you will live a happy life. No one can prevent you from this.

The first rule is to keep an untroubled spirit. The second
is to look at things clearly and seek to know them
for what they are.

If there's something you should do, stop fretting and do it.
If there's nothing you can do, you're not responsible.

Instead of praying to get something or be spared
something, pray that you be freed from lusting
after it or dreading it so much.

Punish your appetites rather than allowing
your appetites to punish you.

Is your piece of fruit bitter? Throw it away.
Are there thorns in your path? Turn aside.
That's enough. Don't go on to complain that things
like this exist in the world.

Once you dismiss the view you're taking,
you're out of danger.
Who then is hindering this dismissal?

Improve people or put up with them.

If someone is doing right, you have no place
being annoyed. If they're doing wrong,
it's almost certainly out of unwitting ignorance.

Our anger at others often wounds us worse
than the things about which we are angry.
Where is the anger for your own lack of
foresight in avoiding the injury?

Approval by itself doesn't improve something.
To expect a special reward for doing your work
is like your eye demanding a reward because it sees,
or your feet because they walk.

A spring will produce fresh water
regardless of whether someone stands nearby cursing it.
Even if filth is thrown into the water,
it soon settles or is washed away.

Pass through this little space of time embracing nature
and spirit, and end your journey in contentment,
just as an olive falls off when it is ripe,
blessing the tree and the sun that produced it.

It is not the weight of the future or
the past that is pressing upon you, but that
of the present alone.

No pain can damage the intelligence.

Nothing is shameful that can
happen to someone good or evil alike.

Nothing happens to any man that he is not
formed by nature to bear.
What we cannot bear removes us from this life.

Time is a river of passing events, and strong
is its current. As soon as a thing is brought forward
it sweeps by and another takes its place,
then this, too, is swept away.

Accept change. You could not have a meal
unless the food underwent change.
Nothing useful happens without change.

To adore anything overmuch is to
fall in love with a beautiful bird that is
even now flying out of sight.

2500 YEARS *of* WISDOM: SAYINGS *of* THE GREAT MASTERS

XII.

჈

from
Epictetus (55-135)

Say what you would be, then get to work.

To be happy and effective in life a person must
distinguish between what is in his control
and what is not. In someone's control is
how he or she relates to the world.
Everything else must be accepted with serenity.

If you focus on something that is not
within your control, you will be neglecting
those things that you are capable of influencing.

Use the resources and opportunities within your grasp.
Do you have books? Learn from them.
Do you have tools? Build with them.

We are all like actors who have been cast in a play.
Divine Will has decided what your role is going to be.
It might be the part of a rich person with physical talents,
or that of a poor person with a severe handicap.

It doesn't matter. It's your job to accept the part
without complaint and to make the most of it.
Give a great performance.

Dare to say to God: "Lead me where you want;
I am of the same mind as you; I am yours and
I accept everything that pleases you."

If you would be good, first believe that you are bad.

Unremarkable lives are held captive by a fear
of not looking capable. Accept that you are a
perpetual beginner, not helpless or irresponsible,
but willing to admit you don't have all the answers.
Admitting weakness is strength.

It is impossible to begin to learn that which one
thinks he already knows.

If you meet with some disappointment, maintain
your tranquility. Say to yourself: "Everything has its
price and this is what I must pay at this moment
for my peace of mind."

If you are faced with an adversity, turn to yourself
and look for the proper resource. If it's a
physical challenge, then stamina is required,
if you encounter an attractive person, then self-restraint
may be called for — if frustrated, patience is needed.

With time, you increase the habit of bringing forth
the appropriate inner resources to deal with each trial,
and the battles are more easily won.

On the occasion of every misfortune that befalls you,
remember to inquire what power you have for
turning this event to use.

The first steps toward a more highly developed life
are the most difficult because of the power of the
fear we have for missing out on pleasures if they aren't
grabbed immediately, and the dread that, if we aspire,
we will be disappointed. As you progress, however,
your resolve will strengthen, and it will eventually
become more and more difficult to work against
your own best interest.

Nothing can be taken from you. Tranquility begins
when we achieve the perspective to say of something not
"I have lost it," but rather, "It has been returned to its source."
Whether something has been taken from you by an
ignorant person or not shouldn't concern you.
What difference does it make who returned it to
the universe. What's important is to gracefully take care
of those things that are currently on loan to us.

Beware faulty logic and associations. For example:
"I am richer than you, therefore, I am better than you."
Whereas the facts only hold: "I am richer than you,
therefore, I have more possessions than you."

It is a sign of growing wisdom to let go of blame.
The more a person works on himself, the less
he tries to grab for easy answers and accepts people
and events for what they are. Others can think
what they think.

When walking, you take care not to step on a nail;
so let it be that you, likewise, mind not
to injure your better sense of yourself.
If someone were to try to make use of your body
in an unhealthy way you would naturally be enraged;
yet people easily give their minds away to
suffer the bad influences of others.

It is not a true expression of friendship to join with
someone in perverse feelings or behavior.
It is of better service to maintain good judgment,
being sympathetic, but leading the way to
a better frame of mind, by example.

Does someone criticize you for being proud or
bad-tempered or greedy or ignorant?
Consider whether their criticisms are true; and,
if they are, correct yourself; if they are not, laugh
and know you're not the person they are criticizing,
but that they dislike an imaginary being.
Perhaps they love what you really are.

People will not see you as you see yourself.
If they do make assumptions about you that
are not true, they simply suffer from ignorance.
Being misunderstood doesn't alter the truth
of who you are. Stop playing to the crowd.

If you find that someone has a criticism of you,
take it with a smile and say: "I'm sure that's true
from their perspective, but they don't know me in full.
Otherwise, they wouldn't have mentioned only
this among my many other faults."
Consider the things you care about and
know that they have a reality that is separate
from how you relate to them.

Assume everything that happens to you
happens for a good reason. That if you
decided to be lucky, you would be lucky.

You are not a child anymore, and you are not
some disinterested bystander to your life. It's time
to stop making excuses and put your beliefs
into action. Participate. The longer you wait,
the more you become weighted down by
mediocrity and insult your better nature.

When you close your door, and darkness is within,
know that you are not alone. God and your sense
of yourself are there. They don't need light
to see what you're doing.

Being good makes possible the greatest of
all things in a life. It allows you to fully inhabit
the present. Instead of squirming around
trying to avoid dealing with constant self-inflicted
shame, looking for escapes or painfully wishing
it were some other way, you can live in this
moment for all its worth.

You are not an isolated unit, but a unique and integral
part of the Universe. It would be ragged and ripped
everywhere if you were not here to read this right now.

DIVINE ARTS

Celebrating the sacred in everyday life

GOODBYE PARKINSON'S, HELLO LIFE!

The Gyro-Kinetic Method for Eliminating Symptoms and Reclaiming Your Good Health

ALEX KERTEN WITH DAVID BRINN

Parkinson's disease, a disorder of the central nervous system, affects 1 million people in America and 10 million worldwide. In *Goodbye Parkinson's, Hello life!* Alex Kerten presents his breakthrough holistic technique that combines dance therapy, behavior modification, and martial arts, to prove that there is life beyond the diagnosis of PD.

"A fascinating hands-on explanation of how movement, music, and mindfulness can replace pills and pain."
—Professor Susan Shapiro, *New York Times* bestselling coauthor
of *Unhooked: How to Quit Anything*

Alex Kerten is founder and director of the Gyro-Kinetics Center in Herzliya, Israel. He has been researching anatomy and the physiology of behavior for over 30 years and treats clients with movement disorders, specializing in Parkinson's disease.

David Brinn is the managing editor of *The Jerusalem Post*, Israel's leading English newspaper.

$18.95 · 200 PAGES · ORDER #GOODBYE · ISBN 9781611250442

Save 25% at **DIVINEARTSMEDIA**.com | **800 833 5738**

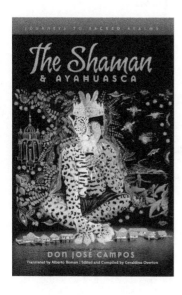

THE SHAMAN & AYAHUASCA
Journeys to Sacred Realms
DON JOSÉ CAMPOS

Internationally respected Peruvian shaman Don José Campos introduces the practices and benefits of Ayahuasca, the psychoactive plant brew used for healing by Amazonian shamans for as long as 70,000 years. Called a plant teacher because it can heal physical, psychological, and emotional blocks, Ayahuasca takes the patient to other realms and dimensions, providing profound insight into our true nature and place in the cosmos.

"This remarkable book suggests a path back to understanding the profound healing and spiritual powers that are here for us in the plant world, reawakening our respect for the natural world, and thus for ourselves."
— John Robbins, author of *Diet for a New America*

$16.95 · 144 PAGES · ORDER #SHAMANBK · ISBN 9781611250039

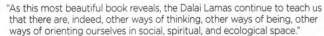

HERE ARE OTHER **DIVINE ARTS** BOOKS YOU MAY ENJOY

DIVINE
ARTS

THE SACRED SITES OF THE DALAI LAMAS
by Glenn H. Mullin

"As this most beautiful book reveals, the Dalai Lamas continue to teach us that there are, indeed, other ways of thinking, other ways of being, other ways of orienting ourselves in social, spiritual, and ecological space."

> — Wade Davis, Explorer-in-Residence, National Geographic Society

THE SHAMAN & AYAHUASCA: Journeys to Sacred Realms
by Don José Campos

"This remarkable and beautiful book suggests a path back to understanding the profound healing and spiritual powers that are here for us in the plant world. This extraordinary book shows a way toward reawakening our respect for the natural world, and thus for ourselves."

> — John Robbins, author, *The Food Revolution* and
> *Diet for a New America*

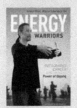

ENERGY WARRIORS
Overcoming Cancer and Crisis with the Power of Qigong
by Bob Ellal and Lawrence Tan

"The combination of Ellal's extraordinary true story and Master Tan's depth of knowledge about the relationship between martial arts and wellness makes for a unique and important contribution to the growing body of literature about holistic thinking and living."

> — Jean Benedict Raffa, author, *Healing the Sacred Divide* and
> *The Bridge to Wholeness*

A HEART BLOWN OPEN:
The Life & Practice of Zen Master Jun Po Denis Kelly Roshi
by Keith Martin-Smith

"This is the story of our time... an absolute must-read for anyone with even a passing interest in human evolution..."

> — Ken Wilber, author, *Integral Spirituality*

"This is the legendary story of an inspiring teacher that mirrors the journey of many contemporary Western seekers."

> — Alex Grey, artist and author of *Transfigurations*

NEW BELIEFS NEW BRAIN:
Free Yourself from Stress and Fear
by Lisa Wimberger

"Lisa Wimberger has earned the right, through trial by fire, to be regarded as a rising star among meditation teachers. No matter where you are in your journey, *New Beliefs, New Brain* will shine a light on your path."

> — Marianne Williamson, author, *A Return to Love* and
> *Everyday Grace*

1.800.833.5738 • 25% discount available online • www.divineartsmedia.com

YEAR ZERO: *Time of the Great Shift*
by Kiara Windrider

"I can barely contain myself as I implode with gratitude for the gift of *Year Zero*! Every word resonates on a cellular level, awakening ancient memories and realigning my consciousness with an unshakable knowing that the best has yet to come. This is more than a book; it is a manual for building the new world!"

— Mikki Willis, founder, ELEVATE

ILAHINOOR: *Awakening the Divine Human*
by Kiara Windrider

"Ilahinoor is a truly precious and powerful gift for those yearning to receive and integrate Kiara Windrider's guidance on their journey for spiritual awakening and wisdom surrounding the planet's shifting process."

— Alexandra Delis-Abrams, Ph.D., author *Attitudes, Beliefs, and Choices*

THE MESSAGE: *A Guide to Being Human*
by LD Thompson

"Simple, profound, and moving! The author has been given a gift... a beautiful way to distill the essence of life into an easy-to-read set of truths, with wonderful examples along the way. Listen... for that is how it all starts."

— Lee Carroll, author, the *Kryon* series; co-author, *The Indigo Children*

SOPHIA—THE FEMININE FACE OF GOD:
Nine Heart Paths to Healing and Abundance

by Karen Speerstra

"Karen Speerstra shows us most compellingly that when we open our hearts, we discover the wisdom of the Feminine all around us. A totally refreshing exploration, and beautifully researched read."

— Michael Cecil, author, *Living at the Heart of Creation*

A FULLER VIEW: *Buckminster Fuller's Vision of Hope and Abundance for All*
by L. Steven Sieden

"This book elucidates Buckminster Fuller's thinking, honors his spirit, and creates an enthusiasm for continuing his work."

— Marianne Williamson, author, *Return To Love* and *Healing the Soul of America*

GAIA CALLS: *South Sea Voices, Dolphins, Sharks & Rainforests*
by Wade Daok

"Wade has the soul of a dolphin, and has spent a life on and under the oceans on a quest for deep knowledge. This is an important book that will change our views of the ocean and our human purpose."

— Ric O'Barry, author, *Behind the Dolphin Smile* and star of *The Cove*, which won the 2010 Academy Award for Best Documentary

Transforming self. Celebrating life.

Divine Arts was created five years ago to share some of the new and ancient knowledge that is rapidly emerging from the indigenous and wisdom cultures of the world; and to present new voices that express eternal truths in innovative and accessible ways.

We have realized from the shifts in our own consciousness that millions of people worldwide are simultaneously expanding their awareness and experiencing the multi-dimensional nature of reality.

Our authors, masters and teachers from around the world, have come together from all spiritual practices to create Divine Arts books. Our unity comes in celebrating the sacredness of life, and having the intention that our work will assist in raising our consciousness which will ultimately benefit all sentient beings.

We trust that these books will serve you on whatever path you journey, and we welcome hearing from you.

Michael Wiese and Geraldine Overton,
Publishers

mw@mwp.com   *glow@blue-earth.co.uk*